CANADIAN SPIES

CANADIAN SPIES

Tales of Espionage in Nazi-Occupied
Europe During World War II

HISTORY

by Tom Douglas

PUBLISHED BY ALTITUDE PUBLISHING CANADA LTD.
1500 Railway Avenue, Canmore, Alberta T1W 1P6
www.altitudepublishing.com
1-800-957-6888

Publisher	Stephen Hutchings
Associate Publisher	Kara Turner
Editor	Debbie Elickson
Digital Photo Colouring	Scott Manktelow

We acknowledge the financial support of the Government
of Canada through the Book Publishing Industry Development
Program (BPIDP) for our publishing activities.

Altitude GreenTree Program
Altitude Publishing will plant twice as many trees as were used
in the manufacturing of this product.

National Library of Canada Cataloguing in Publication Data

Douglas, Tom
Canadian spies / Tom Douglas.

(Amazing stories)
Includes bibliographical references.
ISBN 1-55153-966-7

1. World War, 1939-1945--Secret service--Canada. 2. World War,
1939-1945--Secret service--France. 3. Spies--Canada--Biography.
I. Title. II. Series: Amazing stories (Canmore, Alta.)

D810.S7D68 2003   940.54'8671   C2003-905476-4

An application for the trademark for Amazing Stories™
has been made and the registered trademark is pending.

Printed and bound in Canada by Friesens
2 4 6 8 9 7 5 3

Cover: Canadian forces served throughout Europe
during World War II. These men are stationed in Italy.

To Gail
With fond memories of Brittany
"Whither thou goest, baby!"

Western Europe

Contents

Prologue

Marcel Desjardins knew he was in trouble when the German Army sergeant stepped into the road and held up his hand, signalling Marcel and his travelling companion, Jean-François Guillou, to stop.

Marcel's first problem was the name on his identification papers. He was really Raymond LaBrosse. His companion was Lucien Dumais. They were both Canadian secret agents wearing French civilian clothes. What's more, Raymond was carrying a wireless radio in a suitcase on the back of his bicycle. If the German demanded the suitcase be opened, or realized the papers they were carrying were false, they would be shot as spies.

"We've had it if he finds the radio," Dumais whispered to LaBrosse. "You keep pedalling and I'll see what he wants."

This was no time to argue. LaBrosse steered his bicycle around the German soldier, who made a half-hearted motion to grab at him before Dumais diverted his attention by stopping in front of the German to engage him in an animated conversation.

Canadian Spies

Looking back over his shoulder as he pedalled furiously, LaBrosse saw his fellow countryman waving his arms about and shouting heatedly at the German soldier. Turning his attention back to the road out of Rennes, LaBrosse concentrated on the trip ahead. His orders had been to get to the coast of Brittany as quickly as possible and the bicycle was the fastest means of transport available under the circumstances.

LaBrosse rode with a heavy heart. He was sure he would never see his friend again. But Dumais, who earlier in the war had escaped from a train bound for Germany loaded with Dieppe prisoners of war, still had a few tricks up his sleeve...

Chapter 1
The Fall of France

rank Pickersgill was in the wrong place at the wrong time. A glorious year of post-graduate study in Europe, courtesy of his older brother Jack, ended in a nightmare. September 1939 put him smack in the middle of hostilities when Nazi Germany rolled out its war machine.

When Hitler's Nazis began their conquest of Europe with a lightning strike into Poland, Pickersgill was in Bucharest, Romania. He just managed to find a seat on a crowded train bound for Paris. His next scheduled stop was London, where brother Jack, now Special Assistant to Canadian Prime Minister William Lyon

Mackenzie King, had arranged for him to take his External Affairs oral interview. With a Master's degree in History, and fluency in French and German, Pickersgill was expected to pass the interview with flying colours. This would have led to a prestigious — and safe — job back home in the Canadian civil service. But Pickersgill decided not to keep that appointment.

Frank Herbert Dedrick Pickersgill — Pick to his family and friends — had a stubborn streak a mile wide. He had laboured on road construction projects in his native Manitoba during summer holidays to pay his way through college. In the summer of 1934, he got a job on a cattle boat to England so he could cycle through Britain, France, and Germany. After seeing and hearing the Nazi propaganda machine in full cry during three weeks in Germany in 1938, he wrote a friend about how barbaric and diabolical National Socialism — Nazism — seemed to be.

"I suspect that it will be war this time," he wrote. "It has ceased to have any connection with democracy or any other ideological considerations and it's just a naked question of interest. As a Canadian, I feel like sneering."

Tough Childhood
Pickersgill had good reason for his cynicism. His father

had died in 1920, when Pickersgill was five, of complications from military service in World War I. His family had been forced to move from their Depression-ravaged farm to the city of Winnipeg, where his mother worked as a nurse. During his first travels through Europe, Pickersgill witnessed the early effects of Adolf Hitler's rise to power and became appalled by the rapid advancement of Nazism by the time he revisited Germany in 1938.

"God, what a country," he wrote to a friend. "It was an interesting three weeks but about as depressing as any I've ever spent. The thing is so much worse now than four years ago..."

Convinced that war was inevitable and that Canada would be drawn into the conflict, Pickersgill decided to stay on in Europe and do what he could by reporting on events as they happened.

As a freelance journalist, he was able to get stories placed in such newspapers as *The Winnipeg Free Press*, *The Vancouver Sun*, and Montreal's French-language daily *Le Devoir*. Articles critical of the Nazi regime were also published in *Saturday Night* magazine and the *University of Toronto Quarterly*. His stories were written from Belgium, France, Britain, Italy, Germany, and Romania, as Frank travelled far and wide, interviewing people on their reaction to the growing threat of Hitler's

Nazism. There is no record of Hitler's reaction to the articles, if any, or whether he saw them. But Pickersgill wasn't making any friends in Nazi Germany — and you never knew when you might need a friend.

"When I saw the sloppy, dirty, cheery French customs officers at Kehl, I could have hugged them," Pickersgill wrote. "And then, at Strasbourg, the train filled up and I never would have dreamed that the crowded, noisy disorder could be so glorious. I just sat in the corner of the carriage and grinned and giggled like a loony for about an hour. No wonder these people love their country."

When the German Panzer divisions rumbled into Paris and thousands of hobnailed boots began beating a thunderous tattoo on the cobblestones of the Champs Elysée, Pickersgill was torn between staying and leaving. He believed he could do much good as a Canadian diplomat, but he longed to be right where the action was.

"Please God let me stay in France at least until this war is over," he wrote repeatedly in letters home. This hesitation meant that when he finally decided to go to the Canadian legation in Tours to see about arrangements for getting to England, the legation had already pulled up stakes and headed south. Ironically, the man in charge of the legation was Major-General Georges Vanier, who would one day serve as Canada's Governor-

General at the same time that Pickersgill's brother Jack was a federal Cabinet Minister. Instead of following his fellow Canadians to safety, Pickersgill turned his bicycle — the only means of travel available to him at the time on his meagre income as a freelance journalist — towards the northern French coastal area of Brittany. He wrote to friends that he would find his own way across the English Channel.

Jailed As Enemy Alien
But here his luck ran out. After several weeks of teaching English in the town of Quimper to earn travelling money, Pickersgill was arrested by the Germans as an enemy alien. His journalistic diatribes against the Nazis apparently hadn't gone unnoticed. He was sent to a work camp near Saumur on the Loire River. Hard labour and near-starvation kept him from trying to escape, but then he was moved to a less arduous camp at a former army barracks near Paris.

This was his chance. Armed with a hacksaw smuggled into the camp by a French visitor, Pickersgill and a British prisoner cut their way to freedom. It was March 1942 and Pickersgill had been incarcerated for almost two years. He and his fellow escapee managed to make it south to the unoccupied zone of Vichy France where he was able to secure lodgings in the city of Pau with friends he had made during his earlier travels. He was free — and yet he wasn't.

It would take him six months to obtain an exit visa that allowed him to leave Vichy France and travel to neutral Portugal. The fact that he was a non-combatant — except for the verbal salvos delivered as a journalist — and that he was slightly deaf in one ear, finally convinced the authorities to let him go.

By the time he reached Lisbon in October 1942, Pickersgill had abandoned the idea of becoming a Canadian diplomat — at least until the war was over. He wrote his brother Jack, who was now pleading with him to return to Canada: "…I'm convinced that as far as this war is concerned, there are certain jobs I could do better than anybody, but about a handful of people — and surely that would be the most suitable thing for me to do. That such jobs would be dangerous is just one more thing in their favour…"

Flown to London, Pickersgill pursued contacts in the British Special Operations Executive (SOE) whose mandate was, as British Prime Minister Winston Churchill had put it, to "set Europe ablaze" by working with local activists in Nazi-occupied countries in carrying out acts of sabotage.

By November 1942, Pickersgill was commissioned as a lieutenant in the Canadian Intelligence Corps and attached to SOE the following month. British Intelligence, however, would prove not much friendlier than the Germans. In their rush to get agents into the field, especially those like Pickersgill, who spoke French and were familiar with Occupied France, they cut corners in their preparations for parachuting Pickersgill and his radio operator, John Kenneth Macalister of Guelph, Ontario, into enemy territory.

For instance, rather than outfit the two men with authentic French clothing, they had them buy British garments from second-hand shops, then rip out the linings and rub them with dirt to make them look older and more suitable to the roles the agents would be playing.

Dropped Into France
On the night of June 15, 1943, Pickersgill and his comrade-in-arms parachuted into Occupied France to join SOE's main Paris network, codenamed "Prosper". Unfortunately, it was a unit that expanded too quickly. Its agents, for the most part, were badly trained. It was an Underground operation on the verge of catastrophe.

This time, it was a case of Pickersgill parachuting into the wrong place at the wrong time. Less than a week after being met by members of the Prosper unit, the two Canadians were arrested by the Gestapo and taken to

During World War II both sides operated POW camps.

the infamous Fresnes prison near Paris, where they were brutally interrogated, but refused to give out as much as a scrap of information.

The Fall of France

The incompetence of their SOE handlers turned Pickersgill's desire to help the Allied cause into a cruel twist of fate. In their baggage was a fake parcel to a fictitious prisoner of war in Germany. The packet contained messages to SOE agents in the field — in English — and each was addressed by the individual agent's field name. The Germans lost no time in rounding up the hapless victims of this SOE bungling, along with several hundred members of the French Resistance, great quantities of parachuted arms, and two wireless sets — one of them Macalister's.

But SOE's shoddiness would go even further. Macalister, against all the rules, had been allowed to write down the various codes he would be sending, along with the security checks that would tip off his London handlers if his radio fell into enemy hands. A German officer, who spoke perfect French and a little English, began impersonating Pickersgill and also telegraphed messages back to London on Macalister's radio set, completely fooling the SOE.

The British were so taken in by the ruse, they went along with any request they received from the fake Pickersgill for the next 10 months. In total, 15 large drops of arms and supplies, about $40,000 in French francs, and an unknown number of British and Canadian agents ended up in German hands.

Fate, however, was willing to grant Pickersgill a small measure of revenge. When a captured Canadian agent, Roméo Sabourin, failed to radio London with a prearranged signal indicating that he and a fellow parachutist had landed safely, SOE finally began to suspect that something was amiss amongst the recent batch of agents they had sent in to work behind enemy lines.

They sent a signal to Pickersgill saying they wanted to talk to him in person over an "S" phone. This was an early microwave voice radio with a limited range of about eight to 10 kilometres. This would necessitate the conversation taking place from an aircraft flying over a designated spot, near where the Canadian agent was supposed to be operating.

The Nazis were desperate. Their hoax had been working so well that they would do whatever it took to keep it going — including extricating the real Pickersgill from the Ravitsch concentration camp in Poland, where he had been undergoing periodic torture and constant deprivation for the previous six months.

Pickersgill Goes Berserk

The emaciated Pickersgill, weak from hunger and abuse, was taken by the Gestapo to Paris where he was promised an easy ride for the rest of the war if he would co-operate by talking to the SOE operative over the "S" phone.

The Fall of France

That stubborn streak that had placed Pickersgill in his current situation turned into a violent rage. Not only did he refuse to go along with the Gestapo's request, he somehow found the strength to lurch from his chair, grab a bottle from his interrogator's desk, and club a guard before dashing into a corridor. Confronted by two SS stormtroopers, Pickersgill smashed the bottle against a nearby object and thrust a shard of glass into the throat of one of the onrushing soldiers, severing his jugular vein and killing him instantly. The other soldier was so badly slashed in this unexpected attack that he died two days later in hospital.

Pickersgill ran down the corridor, jumped from a second-floor window, and began to run for cover with SS troops in pursuit. Hit by four bullets, he was recaptured. But he had extracted his revenge — not only by killing two Nazi soldiers, but also by sabotaging the German counter-espionage operation responsible for the capture of Allied agents and the dropping of war materiel into enemy hands.

With Pickersgill refusing to speak to the SOE, the Germans tried to bluff their way through the conversation using the same officer who had been impersonating the captured Canadian agent in dealings with the French Underground. But the man's limited grasp of the English language didn't fool anybody. When the suspicious SOE operative asked for details of Pickersgill's family, the German impersonator was unable to comply. Thus ended the disastrous 10-month hoax.

In agony from his wounds, Pickersgill spent time in a Paris military hospital, then in an SS prison on the Avenue Foch where Macalister was also incarcerated. There they learned of the Allied invasion of Normandy and allowed themselves to hope that they would soon be free. But fate had turned nasty once again.

On August 8, 1944, just two weeks before the liberation of Paris, Pickersgill, Macalister, and Sabourin were shipped to the notorious Buchenwald concentration camp in Germany. That was the beginning of the end.

Once again, Pickersgill found the inner courage to rise above the situation. A British agent, who survived the ordeal, later wrote about the Canadian's superhuman effort to keep everybody's spirits up. In the crowded boxcar taking them to an unknown but ominous fate, Pickersgill told corny jokes in an attempt to take everyone's minds off their situation.

Greeted By Horror

Upon their arrival at the prison camp, the new internees were greeted by a sight straight out of *Dante's Inferno*. The compound was crammed with wide-eyed, starving zombies, rags of clothing hanging from their emaciated bodies, and running sores covering them from head to foot. They howled and wailed at the new arrivals like banshees on a rampage.

Pickersgill again rose to the occasion. He drew his pain-ravaged body to its full six-foot height, threw his shoulders back, and led his small band of fellow prisoners through the maze of human carnage to their barracks, singing and shouting encouragement to those who followed.

This brave Canadian would go to his death showing this same indomitable spirit. On September 6, three weeks after their arrival at what was commonly known as the worst Nazi concentration camp in existence, 15 of the 37 SOE agents, who had arrived in that crammed boxcar, were summoned by loudspeaker to report to the camp's tower area. They never returned to barracks. The next day, a Polish prisoner with contacts in the crematorium squad told the others that the 15 had been executed and their bodies burned.

Three days later, another 16 prisoners received the death call, including Pickersgill, Macalister, and Sabourin.

Remarkably, Pickersgill, limping and staggering from starvation, the pain of his unhealed wounds, and the slight deafness that had plagued him for years, once again led his comrades — this time in a march from which they would never return. Raising his emaciated arms, he began beating time, and in a quavering voice, sang a medley of French, English, and Canadian tunes in march tempo.

But the Nazis would get even for this show of bravado. Pickersgill, Macalister, and Sabourin died an excruciating death. They were hanged from meat hooks anchored to a wall, dying of slow strangulation.

Pickersgill's older brother Jack continued to serve Canadian Prime Minister King and his successor, Louis St. Laurent. He was instrumental in bringing Newfoundland into Confederation and served not only as a Member of Parliament for almost 15 years, but as a federal Cabinet Minister on two different occasions. He died at age 92 in 1997.

It will never be known what would have happened to Frank Pickersgill had he followed in his brother's footsteps and had gone to London for that External Affairs interview.

Perhaps the one legacy he left behind for future generations is a sad testament to the futility, the waste, and the utter insanity of war.

Chapter 2
The Escapers

Sergeant-Major Lucien Dumais of Les Fusiliers Mont-Royal was disgusted with himself. Here he was, a career soldier who had trained hard for the raid on the French coastal town of Dieppe, and now he was crammed into a cattle car with 20 or more bloodied and bedraggled captives on a train bound for a German prison camp. He sneered in the dark and suffocating confines of his rolling prison cell as he remembered the message to the troops the night before from Canadian Major-General "Ham" Roberts: "Don't worry men, it'll be a piece of cake!"

Canadian Spies

The Nazis had been waiting for Dumais and his comrades as they stormed the French beach in the early morning hours of August 19, 1942. Whether British collaborators had reported the build-up of an armada of more than 200 ships in English southern ports or the attack vessels had been spotted ploughing through the choppy waves of the English Channel, the expected victory turned into a rout.

Within nine hours, close to 1,000 young Allied soldiers, the vast majority Canadian and some not even old enough to shave, were cut down by withering machine gun and mortar fire. Twice that many were taken prisoner. Bodies and body parts littered the staging area or floated grotesquely offshore, repeatedly hitting the pebble beach and then sliding back into deeper water with the ebb and flow of the tide.

The carnage disturbed Dumais, but he was a soldier, steeled to such an eventuality. What really bothered him was that he had been forced to surrender in order to save some of the wounded requiring medical attention. And he had indicated his willingness to stop fighting by tying an old khaki handkerchief to the bayonet of his rifle. He couldn't help thinking, as the cattle car rumbled eastward toward the German border, that the hanky, yellow with age, was the colour of cowardice.

But he would be damned if he would spend the rest

of the war behind barbed wire.

He and his fellow Canadian prisoners had marched as stoically as they could out of Dieppe under heavy German guard. Those who could not walk unassisted were half-carried by their comrades. The seriously wounded — and the dead — stayed behind in Dieppe.

The first village reached was St-Martin-L'Eglise. The water the villagers gave them was the first opportunity to quench their thirst since the early morning raid. The locals were friendly and sympathetic. It was obvious they had no love for their German occupiers.

Herded Like Cattle

The prisoners marched all day and well into the night. After a few hours' sleep in a half-constructed factory, they were subjected to intense questioning by German Intelligence. Then they were marched to a railroad siding, where a freight train pulling a long line of cattle cars was idling. The Canadians were ordered to climb aboard.

Before they locked the cattle car Dumais scrambled into, he managed to get a detailed look at the train. One car in three contained guards armed with rifles, machine guns, and sub-machine guns. Getting away seemed impossible, but then so had the thought of anything going wrong on the Dieppe raid.

He and several other escape-minded captives managed to pry one of the planks from the floor of the enclosure. It was an exercise in futility. Just below were the rear wheels of the car. It was evident in the dim light that the axle was too close to the roadbed. There wouldn't be enough clearance should anyone manage to slip through the hole.

They replaced the plank and started working on one of the sheets of wood nailed over the windows on the right side of the cattle car. Once the covering was removed, they saw that a would-be escaper could slip out the window, stand on the narrow walkway outside the car and, at the right moment, jump to freedom — whatever freedom meant for a fugitive Canadian soldier in Nazi-occupied France.

But their whispered plans for escape came to an abrupt halt when they spotted one of the prisoners apparently trying to signal to the guards in the next car through a small window. Dumais dispatched one of his trusted mates to see what that was all about. He came back to report that the fellow claimed to be from Glasgow and belonged to No. 6 Commando Group.

His interrogator spoke perfect English. He reported to Dumais that the fellow's English was atrocious. There was no trace of a Scottish accent and he spoke no French. Furthermore, a check with some of the others in the car led to the conclusion that no commandos from Sixth Company had taken part in the raid. The man was obviously a German spy who must have struggled ghoulishly into the uniform of one of the dead soldiers lying on the beach.

The immediate consensus was to knock the infiltrator unconscious and drop his body through the hole in the floor of the car. But that would mean reprisals from the guards if they found out. It was decided to keep a close watch on the man and if he gave any trouble, someone would throttle him quietly. There would be no shortage of volunteers for the task.

Moment Of Truth Arrives

While these life-and-death discussions were going on, a chance to escape suddenly presented itself. The train began to slow down as it negotiated a sharp curve to the left. This meant the window was probably hidden from the coaches in front of and behind their car. Dumais and two companions were out the opening in a flash. Just then, however, the tracks straightened out and the train began to pick up speed. Jumping at that point would be suicidal.

Dumais' blood ran cold as he saw the lights of a village ahead. They passed through a small station with German soldiers on the platform. The three escapers pressed themselves against the side of the car, certain that all eyes were on them and it would only be a matter of seconds before the alarm went up. But nothing happened. The train kept going. Unbelievably, the same scenario was played out a second time, with the same results. Finally, the train slowed down again on a steep grade and the three men jumped off, rolling and tumbling down an embankment.

Hitting a ditch at the bottom, Dumais sprang to his feet and began running away from the direction of the train. This time, he was spotted and bullets screamed by his head as he ran a zigzag pattern along the gully. When he reached a dense clump of bushes, he dived into them and held his breath. There was no sound but that of the train receding into the distance. He was certain a search party, complete with snarling Alsatian guard dogs, would soon be after him. But time inched by and nothing happened.

Finally, Dumais continued his trek along the ditch, from time to time whistling the first few bars of an old French Canadian song *Un Canadien Errant*, which was his regimental bugle call and would have been instantly recognized by his two erstwhile companions. It received no response. They had probably gone in a different direction. He began to jog along the ditch, strangely elated. He was alone on French soil, still in his Canadian

Army uniform, surrounded by the enemy and without resources. But he was free.

Once the adrenaline churned up by his escape had burned off, his body began to make the usual demands. There had been no drinking water since that little village just outside Dieppe and he was experiencing a burning thirst. Nature, at that moment, decided to step in and provide him with a fresh stream he heard gurgling as he loped along. He drank his fill, then stripped off his uniform, and bathed in the chilly water. He rinsed his clothes as best he could to rid them of the salt from the seawater of Dieppe and then shivered back into them.

Nature's Banquet

Next, he discovered a fruit orchard where he gorged on apples and pears, stuffing a few into his tunic for later. He still had half a loaf of German bread saved as emergency rations. His luck held and he soon came to a tiny village where one small house stood apart from the others. There was a barn out back and he silently crept into the hayloft.

Fatigued from his ordeal, he fell into a quick sleep. As he drifted off, he began planning how he would make his way to the English Channel, steal a boat, and row to freedom.

Next morning, in the cold, grey light of dawn, he

decided he would have to have help if his escape plan was to work. He spoke French and knew from escape lectures before the abortive raid on Dieppe that very few French natives were familiar with the language of French Canada. They would most likely assume anyone speaking with that dialect was one of the hundreds of transient workers from other parts of France who roamed the countryside.

But even a simpleton would recognize a Canadian Army uniform. Stealing clothes would be difficult and dangerous. He would have to rely on rumours about how much the rural French inhabitants hated the Germans.

Dumais' luck held. He decided to knock on the door of a big house across the street. The young woman who answered was momentarily taken aback by his dishevelled appearance, but as she later revealed, news about the Dieppe raid was on the radio. She guessed Dumais was a casualty of that unsuccessful expedition and told him to wait a minute while she checked to make sure he hadn't been spotted by anyone else. He decided to give her five minutes before he turned and fled. The woman was back before his arbitrary deadline. He had not been seen. She invited him in and gave him food and wine.

It soon became apparent the woman, Madame

Collai, was used to helping fugitives flee the Nazis. She told him to take off his boots and uniform. Her gardener, who identified himself as Robert, pulled the hobnails out of the boots — they were a dead give-away that he was a soldier. Having no other shoes for him, they smeared the boots with mud to make them look more like those a farmer would wear. Next came a beret, a threadbare shirt, and pants several sizes too big.

Dumais was overwhelmed with gratitude. There were notices plastered on fences and building walls threatening the death penalty to anyone aiding an escapee. Madame Collai had three small children, yet she was determined to assist him.

Plan Doomed To Failure

She and her gardener insisted that the plan to head for the English Channel and row to safety in a stolen boat was bound to fail. The coast was a heavily fortified military area that required special passes. All boats were under lock and key. And the Channel was a treacherous stretch of water. He would have a much better chance if he headed south towards Poitiers, where he could cross over the demarcation line between Occupied France and the relatively neutral Vichy zone. From there, it would be possible to take a boat to the British colony of Gibraltar on Spain's southern tip.

Their arguments prevailed and the next day he prepared to take his leave. Once again, Madame Collai was more than generous, giving Dumais a razor, soap, and a map of France torn out of one of her children's geography books. This remarkable woman then handed over precious bread coupons and most of the money she had on hand.

Making his way to the train station, Dumais mumbled a request for a third-class ticket to Poitiers. He was still uncomfortable in his hand-me-down costume and found it awkward speaking a dialect that was full of pitfalls. The language of French Canada contained many anglicized words that would be a dead give-away. He received the ticket and change without incident.

The next heart-stopping moment occurred as he boarded the train and met head-on with a German soldier. It was the first such encounter since Dumais' escape. Their eyes met and his heart raced. The soldier looked away and Dumais was able to relax. But not for long. Reaching Le Mans, the train stopped to allow a troop of German soldiers to board. They began going through the train asking people for their identity papers. Dumais managed to slip out an exit without being seen and again set out on foot.

After plodding several kilometres under a hot sun and concealing himself in ditches or behind bushes whenever any vehicles approached, Dumais decided to chance it once again by revealing himself to the occupants of a small farm. They took him in, giving him a chunk of bread and a bowl of coffee. But the farmer's wife didn't trust Dumais, thinking he might be an *agent provocateur* — a French collaborator who would turn her and her husband in for being willing to harbour a fugitive.

Dumais heard the whispered argument, almost chuckling at the irony of being thought of as a German plant. He was only too happy to comply when the woman finally asked him to leave. He didn't want any fuss. As a peace offering, the farmer's wife sent him on his way with a bacon sandwich and some hardboiled eggs.

At the next small train station, Dumais boarded a train for Tours, arriving without incident. As he stepped down onto the platform, he helped a woman struggling with several large suitcases. Throughout the course of their conversation, he learned that she was on her way to Poitiers and lived close to the demarcation line. During the hour's wait for the connecting train, Dumais quizzed her, trying to be as casual as possible so as not to raise her suspicions.

Once again, he was thought to be someone other than who he really was. The woman took him for a

Frenchman who had escaped from a German work camp. He decided to play along.

More Acts Of Kindness
Arriving at Poitiers late at night, Dumais said goodbye to his informative travelling companion. With no one in the station, he slept on a hard bench. At daybreak, he set off on foot for the Free Zone. Reaching another small village, Dumais decided to trust to luck once again. He stopped at a farm and asked for a glass of water. The woman who answered the door told him to wait while she fetched her husband from his blacksmith forge.

The heavily built blacksmith, when he learned who Dumais was, grasped his hand and began to shake it vigorously. He knew about the Dieppe Raid and peppered Dumais with questions: When would the real Invasion begin? Dumais really didn't know and said so. How had the fugitive managed to travel some 400 kilometres in just five days? Dumais was stunned at the realization that the attack had occurred on August 19, and this was only August 24. He told his questioner his luck, so far, was owed to the kindness of a number of locals risking their lives for him.

The blacksmith wanted to join the ranks of Dumais' benefactors, offering to take him across the demarcation line. Dumais talked him out of it. He had already done enough. The man insisted on drawing a map showing guard posts, including a German machine-gun nest up in a tree right at the border.

Just then, an old man and his grandson arrived by horse-drawn cart to pick up some machinery repaired by the blacksmith. They agreed to take Dumais part of the way, dropping him off a few kilometres from the line where he spent the rest of the day in a ditch waiting for dark.

After all his adventures, the crossing into Unoccupied France was without incident — which led to Dumais letting down his guard for a few minutes. In the dark, he almost bumped into a soldier with a rifle pointed at him. Disregarding the order to halt, Dumais quickly marched backwards about 10 paces, then turned and ran. Once again, bullets whistled by his ears as he reached another ditch and ran as fast as he could, putting several kilometres between himself and the soldier. Had he been French or German? Dumais hadn't thought it wise to ask.

But his luck still held. After a night spent sleeping in a haystack, Dumais heard a car approaching. The couple in the automobile offered him a lift. After giving them the once-over, he accepted. They took him to Lussac-les-Châteaux, where a band of Resistance fighters provided him with identity papers and passed him along a human chain to the coastal city of Marseilles, then on to Perpignan with several other escapers. A short train ride took them to Canet-Plage near the Spanish border.

Sailors In Disguise

One more surprise was in store for Dumais as he and his fellow escapers were rowed out to a Portuguese fishing trawler bound for Gibraltar and freedom. They were on the open sea before they discovered that the small, weather-beaten vessel was actually a Royal Navy ship.

Despite a few close calls where patrolling German warships challenged the "trawler", their ruse held and they eventually reached Gibraltar. From there, it was an uneventful trip back to London.

Dumais was told that, as compensation for experiencing such hardships, he could now look forward to a cushy desk job for the rest of the war. Everyone marvelled at his ability to travel from the north coast of France to the south, through hostile territory. They were also impressed at the number of brave French people risking torture and death to help him escape.

His knowledge of France and his experiences in avoiding capture by a pursuing enemy had not, however, been lost on the SOE. After he had been debriefed about his exploits, he was stunned to be asked by British

Intelligence to return to France and set up an escape network for the increasing numbers of downed pilots, escaped POWs and agents whose time had run out.

Dumais thought back to all the people who had come to his assistance, and to the fear, and then relief experienced on his flight to freedom. He remembered his disgust at surrendering under a yellowed hankie. He recalled the cries of anguish from his wounded comrades. His mind filled with memories of the swaggering Nazi bullies laughing mockingly as they herded him and the other captives into the cattle cars and rolled the heavy doors shut.

He wanted to go on fighting, that was certain. But he was sorely tempted to rejoin his regiment and experience the visceral thrill of close-quarter combat. Still, he realized there was a crying need for people with his language capabilities and experience to parachute into Occupied France and help others escape. He would need some time to think about his next course of action.

One thing was for certain. He would never be satisfied sitting out the rest of the war behind a desk in London.

Gabriel Chartrand

Gabriel Chartrand knew he would have to escape in the next few minutes or he would be a goner. He remembered from his espionage training that if captured by the Gestapo, you had to get out of their clutches before you ended up at German headquarters. Once the doors slammed behind you, all you had to look forward to was excruciating torture, and if you were lucky, an early death. Your heart would give out from the pain your body was being subjected to. Your interrogator would misjudge the intensity of the torture he was administering and kill you accidentally. Or the Nazis would decide you were expendable because you either didn't possess the information they sought or your pain threshold was such that they would never extract it from you.

That was the good news. But if your body was strong, you would survive all these horrors and be forced to endure them time after agonizing time for weeks or perhaps months. Then, according to the reports of the few French Resistance fighters who managed to escape from Gestapo torture chambers, you were accorded a spy's death — by gas chamber, garrotting, or a bullet to the back of the neck.

No matter what the scenario, one thing you knew for certain. You lost any advantage you might have once they took you inside.

Several Close Calls
Joseph Gabriel Chartrand, or Gaby as he was commonly

known, was the third Canadian into France in 1943. There were a number of close calls. The Underground networks Chartrand was working with were systematically betrayed and their members arrested, so he had to switch identity papers several times. Like his friend and fellow agent, Guy Bieler, Chartrand was a fatalist who believed he was going to die when his number came up, and nothing could change that fact. However, he just as firmly believed that you didn't have to help the Grim Reaper along by giving up without a fight.

So here he was walking along a sidewalk in Tours beside a member of the Gestapo who was pointing a pistol at him. Chartrand, whose survival depended on knowing such things, was aware that the German interrogation centre was just down the street.

Actually, things had improved one hundred per cent in the last few minutes, which gave the captured Canadian reason for optimism. He had, in fact, been arrested by two Gestapo agents while pedalling his bicycle back into the city after successfully getting a downed American flier into a countryside safe house. With the German agents waiting for him on the street leading to his apartment, it seemed certain that another Resistance cell had been compromised.

Perhaps enemy agents or collaborators had managed to infiltrate the network. Maybe one of the cell members had slipped up. Or it could be one of those random acts of fate that no amount of planning could foresee. He tried to ignore the obvious. His section chief's mistress was insanely jealous — which Chartrand found strange since he had good reason to know that she wasn't exactly lily-white herself. Could she have betrayed the cell to spite her lover? Chartrand gave a mental shrug and brought himself back to the present. There were more immediate problems to solve.

One of the Gestapo thugs had insisted Chartrand deflate the tires of his bicycle but, perhaps thinking of confiscating the bike and selling it on the black market, had allowed him to wheel it along the sidewalk on his way to interrogation at German headquarters. Stroke of luck number one. A bicycle wasn't much of a weapon, but it was better than nothing.

One Down And One To Go

His spirits rose again when the second Gestapo agent spotted someone on a side street he thought was another member of the Resistance. He told his companion to keep heading for their headquarters and he took off in hot pursuit of the suspect. That left Chartrand alone with just one captor. Lucky happenstance number two.

As he waited for his chance to flee, Chartrand thought back to the instructions given at espionage school in England. If a fugitive could get 15 long strides on his captor, his chances for escape escalated considerably. Even if the adversary were armed, he would have a better chance of hitting the fleeing captor by throwing his pistol at him than he would by shooting at a dodging and weaving target on the run.

Chartrand also thought of his friend, Guy Bieler, who was probably also somewhere in Occupied France at the moment. Bieler was a fellow Montrealer who had served with Chartrand's older brother Paul, in the Régiment de Maissoneuve in England. Chartrand, who was 32 when war broke out in 1939, immediately enlisted in the Royal Montreal Regiment. Considered too old for infantry officer's training school, he ended up in England as a statistics clerk with the rank of sergeant at Canadian Military Headquarters in London. During a visit with his brother Paul, Chartrand became reacquainted with Bieler and they shared memories about their days in Montreal.

It wasn't long before Chartrand confessed his boredom and frustration to Bieler. His friend seemed to brighten at this revelation, then told him to be patient; he would put in a good word for him with some very important people who might have a more interesting job for him.

Almost immediately, Chartrand was contacted by

the SOE, interrogated, and accepted for training as a saboteur in Occupied France. A leg injury during parachute training prevented him from jumping to his destination. Instead, he was flown over the Channel in a Lysander on the night of April 14, 1943, and along with one other fellow agent, was turned over to the care of a Resistance unit in the meadows of the Loire Valley.

Lysander pilots were trained to land, offload their cargo — human or otherwise — and be airborne again within minutes. The sound of the retreating aircraft told Chartrand his days of boring work as a statistics clerk were long behind him and the exciting, dangerous life of a saboteur was underway.

The next few months were spent building up the local Resistance network, instructing its members in the use of Sten guns, arranging for supply drops, and assisting in the sabotage of rail lines. Then came the request to help a hidden Missouri airman to a farmhouse from where he would be passed along the escape network and returned safely to England...

Running Out Of Time

Chartrand's thoughts were interrupted by the realization that he was only about 300 metres from Gestapo headquarters. If he was going to get out of the jam he was in, something needed to happen soon.

Just then, an opportunity presented itself. A street ran off to his right and he was wheeling his bicycle on his left side, having made sure to position it between himself and his less-than-alert German captor. It was now or never. Picking up the bicycle, he hurled it with all his might at the Gestapo agent, knocking him to the ground.

Chartrand began to run down the side street as fast as he could, pistol shots ricocheting off the sidewalk and buildings like angry wasps carrying deadly venom. He would later tell friends he surely must have beaten the world's record that day for the 500-metre dash.

With only the clothes on his back and a little money in his pockets, Chartrand made his way to Paris where he tried to contact his superior by telephoning the apartment of the man's mistress. When a German-accented male voice answered the call, Chartrand's heart sank. Like some badly written soap opera, a jealous lover must have turned her paramour over to the authorities. And to add insult to injury, she was apparently collaborating with the enemy if, as Chartrand suspected, that voice on the phone was that of a German officer.

Chartrand didn't need any more warning signs. It was time he got out of France. But how? He was almost broke. His identity papers were useless and his colleagues seemed to be in worse straits than he was.

Chartrand and his fellow agents knew you could learn the espionage rulebook by heart and take all the precautions in the world, but if you didn't have luck on your side, you were doomed from the start. His luck now took a turn for the better. Wandering along the Champs Elysées, trying to think of his next move, he literally bumped into a man he recognized from an earlier operation. His newly rediscovered benefactor was a member of a *maquis* — a cell of the French Resistance — who hid him in a safe house in Paris. After several weeks, Chartrand was moved to another Parisian safe house. It was the policy of the French Underground not to keep fugitives in one spot for too long.

As the weeks passed, Chartrand helped a downed Royal Australian Air Force squadron leader reach an escape line, then returned to the Paris flat to await further developments. Finally, in late autumn, Chartrand, along with two Free French agents and a young U.S. air force gunner, was moved to Rennes. The men waited while arrangements were being made to get them to the Normandy coast, where a pick-up by the Royal Navy would see them safely back in England.

Disguised As French Workers
Just at the point when they thought they would go out of

their minds with boredom, Chartrand and his cooped-up companions were moved to a village in Normandy, about 30 kilometres from the coast. There, disguised as French workers, the four fugitives set to work, repairing a run-down flourmill while awaiting arrangements for safe passage across the English Channel.

After 10 days at the mill, its owner took the fugitives to the coast. A hazardous climb down a rocky cliff would provide a midnight rendezvous at a designated beach with a Royal Navy motor gunboat from Dartmouth. However, Chartrand's luck faded a bit, at a very inconvenient moment. As he and his companions clung to the cliff, flares suddenly turned the midnight-shrouded coast into broad daylight. It was back to Dartmouth for the Royal Navy vessel and all the way back to Rennes for Chartrand and his fellow escapers.

At last, on the night of December 9, Chartrand and his three companions were taken back to the beach and were loaded into two small rubber boats, manned by Royal Navy personnel. The boats were rowed out into the Channel where the fugitives were offloaded onto a motor gunboat and whisked to freedom in England.

The days fraught with heart-pumping danger were over for Chartrand. He was too well known by the Gestapo to return to Occupied France. He would have to settle for a routine desk job from this point onward.

While he did return to France for a year or so after the Liberation of Paris, as a censor working with the French press, the greatest risk he faced in that job was a paper cut.

Not until the war was over and security measures loosened did Chartrand learn that his rescue from a small beach in Normandy was the prototype for a much larger operation to the west on the coast of Brittany. Close to 150 Allied servicemen and escaping British agents followed in his footsteps to freedom across the English Channel.

Chapter 3
Grandad Guy

G ustav "Guy" Bieler had several good reasons to excuse himself from military service when World War II broke out in September 1939. First of all, he was in his mid-30s — well past the age of most of the young men and women accepting the challenge to fight "for King and country". Bieler was also a married man with a wife and two small children to support. As chief of translation for the Sun Life Assurance Company of Canada in Montreal, he could legitimately claim his work was essential to the war effort.

He could have fallen back on the fact that his

parents were Swiss. Switzerland had a centuries-old tradition of staying neutral while war raged outside its borders. True, Bieler himself had been born in France and settled in Canada in 1924, at the urging of an uncle who taught at McGill University. France and Canada had declared war on Nazi Germany after Adolf Hitler sent troops and civilian-strafing divebombers into Poland. But Bieler could still have clung to that Swiss heritage.

If that hadn't been justification enough to keep him from donning the khaki uniform of a Canadian soldier, he could always have claimed, as a number of his fellow Quebecers were doing at the time, that the battles raging in Europe were not really Canada's war. Why volunteer to fight and probably die in a far-off land across the sea just because some madman had picked a fight with the Poles?

Bieler enlisted anyway, later telling a colleague: "You cannot permit what these Germans are doing to spread. I have people in France — my brother and others. I want to help save people from being pushed around."

Bieler signed up with the University of Montreal unit of the Canadian Officers Training Corps within weeks of the declaration of war. He was commissioned a lieutenant in le Régiment de Maisonneuve in June 1940. Three months later, the pipe-smoking, mild-mannered music lover had kissed his wife and small children goodbye and sailed to England within the cramped confines of a troop ship.

Everyone Liked Guy
Bieler's calm yet resolute demeanour brought him instant respect from his comrades. He was soon made the regiment's intelligence officer, taking part in plans for defending Great Britain against an expected German landing on England's south coast. This assignment led to a chance meeting with Colonel Maurice Buckmaster, a former Ford salesman in France, who was heading up SOE's French Section. Buckmaster's selling powers were such that in June 1942, Bieler left the Maisonneuves and was sent to Wanborough Manor, SOE's "preparatory school" in Surrey.

Next stop was Arisaig in Scotland, where he spent a month acquiring skills in unarmed combat, knife fighting, pistol and machine-gun firing, map reading, and telegraphy. Then came training in parachuting and an advanced course in espionage.

His passion for canoeing in the wilds of Québec had prepared him well for the rigorous training at the spy school. He never complained, and he was the first to volunteer for assignments. At 38, he was older by at least a decade than most of the others in his class, who

affectionately called him "Grandad". But the commanding officer at Wanborough would write in his journals
that Bieler was "...the best student we've had. He is
conscientious, keen, intelligent, a sound judge of char-
acter; good-natured, absolutely reliable, outstandingly
thorough, a born organizer."

Gabriel Chartrand, a sergeant in the Maisonneuves
who knew Bieler and followed in his footsteps by heading into Occupied France as a saboteur, later reported
that the Wanborough CO told him: "If you're half as
good as Guy, you'll be magnificent."

Bieler's sister, Madelaine Dale, and her husband,
Hartas, were probably the only people to know that
Bieler would soon be leaving England for parts
unknown. On the evening of November 10, 1942, Bieler
arrived at the Dale household in the London suburb of
Ewell to have dinner — as he had done on many occasions since arriving in England. Only this time, for the
first time, he was wearing civilian clothes instead of the
uniform of a captain in the Canadian Army.

Mrs. Dale later recounted that while Bieler would
not talk about the future, she inspected his overcoat as
she was hanging it up. The labels had been removed.
She suspected this meant he was a spy and was making
his last visit to her home.

Grandad Guy

Prepares To Jump

On the evening of November 18, 1942, eight days after an emotional farewell with his sister, Bieler reported to Tempsford aerodrome in preparation for parachuting into Occupied France. He had a final briefing with Vera Atkins, head of intelligence with the SOE's "F" section. She possessed a storehouse of knowledge about life across the Channel — curfews, rationing, travel restrictions, required documentation, surveillance, and security checks.

Atkins also reminded Bieler of the many risks he faced, but even she wasn't fully aware of just how dangerous a situation he was getting himself into. After the war, it was revealed that of 480 agents SOE sent into France, 130 were captured — a more than one-third failure rate. Of those 130 captured, only 26 survived.

Atkins remembered Bieler's mature outlook, his calm kindness and poise — and his beautiful voice. She would later refer to him as "a man among boys".

Unfortunately, a rocky patch of ground southwest of Paris provided a major setback to the plans "F" section had for its star pupil — although his determined spirit would see him overcome severe pain and carry out acts of superhuman courage and cunning.

Landing heavily on a rocky outcropping after parachuting from a Whitley bomber with two other agents,

Bieler suffered a bad back injury. He was immobilized for hours, but somehow his companions, Captain Michael Trotobas and an English wireless operator, Lieutenant A.A.G. Staggs, managed to move him several kilometres to the village of Auxy-Iuranville. Then they all took a train to Paris.

Allied agents in Occupied France relied on a network of "safe houses" — homes and apartments volunteered by members of the French Resistance — from which they could carry on their clandestine operations. Bieler's fellow saboteurs led him to such a sanctuary on Paris's Boulevard de Suffren. So severe was the damage to Bieler's spine that he spent six weeks in a Paris hospital, using false identity papers in the name of Guy Morin. This was followed by three months' recuperation in another safe house near the Eiffel Tower.

Once again Bieler had a perfect opportunity to put himself on the sidelines and let others fight the war. The SOE sent a signal, offering to fly him out of enemy territory to a safe desk job back in London. Bieler absolutely refused.

Trotobas and Staggs had gone on to set up a sabotage network at Lille, a city in Northern France that had been the scene of fierce fighting in World War I. Bieler's assignment was to organize a similar *réseau* in St. Quentin, a city of some 60,000 inhabitants, about

Grandad Guy

130 kilometres northeast of Paris.

Recruits While Injured
Working on the premise of better late than never, Bieler finally arrived at the St. Quentin railway station in early April 1943. He was met by Eugène Cordelette, a land surveyor and leader of the local Underground Resistance unit. Cordelette was shocked to see Bieler limping along the platform in obvious poor health and great pain. For the next week, the Canadian agent could do little except sit in a chair in Cordelette's back yard in the village of Fonsomme, dressed in the ubiquitous French worker "uniform" of blue smock and trousers. But he put the time to good use, interviewing and recruiting agents for his sabotage unit. Their assignment was to receive arms by parachute drop and train others for local insurrection when the Allies eventually invaded France.

His network was codenamed "Musician". Bieler loved to relax back home in Montreal by playing the piano and listening to classical recordings. The group's membership was soon large enough and so skilled in the tactics of sabotage to become a major impediment to the Nazi war machine.

Finding the strength to lead the unit, Bieler directed his men — mostly railway workers who knew strategic targets — in acts of mayhem. He could still stand for only a few hours a day and moved with his head to one side, one shoulder hunched from the severe pain along his spine. Despite his condition, Bieler oversaw acts of sabotage that destroyed a German troop train, derailed 20 other trains, damaged 20 locomotives by applying a special lubricant that actually wore out parts quickly, wrecked an engine repair shop and 11 other locomotives, and cut the Paris-Cologne rail line 13 times.

As always, Bieler's resolute spirit and sense of fair play greatly impressed his colleagues. Cordelette would later comment that Bieler was distraught whenever he heard of civilian casualties from Allied bombing raids on railway lines, perhaps thinking of his wife and two small children back home in Montreal. He sent messages back to London, asking that rail sabotage be left to his network.

"On one occasion," Cordelette recalled, "to avoid loss of civilian lives, he refused to blow up an important munitions train on a siding near many houses. He made up for this by having another munitions convoy blown up in the uninhabited countryside."

Shades Of Sherwood Forest
In another instance, Bieler took on the role of a Canadian Robin Hood. With food scarce, he organized a burglary of the town hall of Vaux-en-Digny in order to

feed his agents and the local populace. The food coupons taken in the raid were distributed to those most in need.

To add to his physical pain, Bieler received a cruel emotional blow that November when he learned of the death of Trotobas, the parachutist who had helped him to safety when he had injured his back. Betrayed by a captured agent, Trotobas was shot in a dawn gunfight with the Gestapo. Drawing upon what seemed to be an inexhaustible well of determination, Bieler took on the added task of helping to keep the Lille network going, as well as his own.

His load, however, was lessened considerably with the arrival of a wireless operator codenamed "Mariette" — a 32-year-old Anglo-Swiss woman in the Women's Auxiliary Air Force, whose real name was Yolande Beekman. Until she was attached to Bieler's network, he had been forced to rely on using wireless operators from other cells to exchange messages with the SOE. This arrangement was not only inconvenient but dangerous because he had no way of knowing whether these other networks had been infiltrated by the Gestapo, as many were.

St. Quentin was an important link in the canal system that threads through France, from the northeast all the way south to the Mediterranean. The Germans were using the canals to transport supplies, including submarine parts made in Rouen. Destroying this strategic material would hamper the effectiveness of the German U-boat fleet that was devastating Allied shipping, both naval vessels and merchant ships.

Royal Air Force bombers had blasted the canal locks to little effect. They next dropped underwater limpet time bombs in cargo canisters, retrieved by Bieler's network. Despite the excruciating pain in his back, Bieler, accompanied by two assistants, lay flat in the bottom of a drifting punt to make it appear abandoned. When the boat reached a principal lock gate, the saboteurs placed three waterproof bombs below the waterline and set the timing devices to allow themselves to get safely away. The mines, quite literally, were a thundering success. Next, these explosives were used to destroy 40 loaded barges, the detonations timed for when the canals were jammed with watercraft. Barge traffic was delayed for several weeks as the Germans struggled to clear away the debris.

No one knew Bieler by his real name. He was simply Commandant Guy to everyone with whom he came into contact. The Germans were enraged by the effectiveness of his leadership in destroying vital war materiel. The Gestapo was under extreme pressure to uncover this highly successful band of saboteurs and send them to their deaths after extracting every last scrap of information from them by torture.

Wireless Operations Risky

SOE agents knew that more arrests came from the detection of wireless operators than by the infiltration of enemy counteragents. Bieler and Beekman took whatever evasive action they could, aware that it was only a matter of time before the German technicians zeroed in on them.

But moving a cumbersome transmitter and finding different safe houses in which to set it up, without their movements being reported by the many collaborators who riddled every city, town and village in France, was a daunting task. It was hard to decide just when it was safe to stay in one place and when it was time to move on.

By all accounts, Bieler should actually have been pulled out of France after six months in the field — the average survival time for a saboteur. But the SOE, pleased with his work and anxious to rack up even more clandestine victories in preparation for the impending Allied invasion, left him there long after his own personal doomsday clock had reached midnight.

Agent Chartrand, who followed Bieler into the world of sabotage, would later recall his colleague talking to him about the dangers of going up against the

German Gestapo and SS: "We probably have a 50–50 chance of coming out alive," Bieler told his friend, adding that he was a fatalist. "I'm going to die the day I'm going to die."

In October, radio operator Beekman began transmitting from the attic of a house in St. Quentin. One day in December, she spotted a German car in the neighbourhood with wireless detection equipment protruding from its roof. The radio was moved to the home of another Resistance fighter, Camille Boury.

Boury and his wife hosted a Christmas party for Bieler and Beekman. Boury would later recall: "Guy arrived carrying two Père Noëls stuffed with candy for our children and under each arm a few good bottles. We listened to the BBC messages from London and then the wonderful Christmas music. We had the traditional pine tree. Guy recited to us (as he could so well) the beautiful poetry of Verhaeren and Victor Hugo. We sang Canadian and French choruses."

Boury also remembered that at midnight, Guy became very quiet, putting his head in both hands for a long time. When he finally looked up, he seemed distraught and asked for a pencil. On the back of a photograph he wrote: "Chief, French Dept., Sun Life Assurance Company, Dominion Square, Montreal." He said to the Bourys: "If misfortune overtakes me, write to this address. You will find my wife there. Tell her how I spent Christmas. Describe this evening to her. Tell her how I thought of them."

Then, as he had done on many occasions, he asked to see the Bourys sleeping children, a young son and daughter of about the same age as his own children. He stood there looking at the youngsters for quite a while, then quietly called it an evening.

Time Runs Out

The year 1944 was little over a week old when a stranger was spotted in the street outside the Boury house. His coat collar was turned up and seemed to be concealing a set of earphones. Bieler and Beekman felt the noose tightening. On January 15, the two agents were relaxing in one of their local haunts, the Café du Moulin Brulé on a secluded road near the St. Quentin Canal. Suddenly, two cars screeched to a halt outside the building and a dozen armed Germans stormed through the doors. Bieler and his wireless operator were arrested, along with the café's owners.

It was a well-planned raid. In all, 40 members of the network were rounded up, including Cordelette, the land surveyor who had housed Bieler when he first arrived in the area. The night he was arrested, Cordelette saw a badly beaten Bieler in a corridor of the

St. Quentin Prison being taken to a small cell after the first of what would be countless brutal interrogations by the Gestapo.

"He was chained hand and foot," the land surveyor would recall later. "His face was horribly swollen, but I could read in his eyes this order: 'Whatever happens, don't talk!' In spite of all torments, he showed no weakness."

Bieler's silence, in part, was because of an SOE training session, in which it had been pointed out that, if a captured agent remained silent for 48 hours, it would give other members of his network a chance to escape. But his main impetus was an abiding disdain for Nazism and a resolve to protect his loved ones at all costs. Ironically, his beloved brother René-Maurice, an active Resistance fighter, would die in a concentration camp in February 1945 — the victim of an Allied bombing raid.

A citation for a Distinguished Service Order award, that was made later on Bieler's behalf, praised his fortitude: "Despite the most barbarous forms of torture by the enemy over a period extending over at least eight days, he refused absolutely to divulge the names of any one of his associates, or the location of any arms dumps. Despite the intense pain that he was suffering from the injury to his back, he faced the Gestapo with the utmost determination and courage."

Bieler's steadfast refusal to give out any information paid dividends for the Allied cause. Six months later, when the invasion of Normandy began, several of Bieler's sabotage and ambush squads were still intact. They performed deeds of bravery that hampered the arrival of German reinforcements on the besieged beaches of Northern France.

Sent To A Hellhole
Three months of interrogation followed Bieler's initial arrest. His back injury worsened and one of his kneecaps was broken. Still he refused to talk. In disgust, his interrogators sent him off to the infamous Flossenburg concentration camp in Bavaria, where he was locked up in a tiny, concrete, windowless cell. To add starvation to the agony he suffered from his injuries, he was forced to subsist on a watery soup and a tasteless lump of what passed for bread.

Finally, on September 9, 1944 — a little over three months after the Allies had gained a toehold in Europe by their successful D-Day landings — Bieler heard the cadence of heavy boots in the corridor outside his cell. Bracing for the worst, he was surprised to find a German honour guard, rifles on their shoulders, waiting for him. As with so many others who found Bieler to be a remarkable human being, his jailers and interrogators were impressed by his quiet resolve and grace under torture. They had decided not to execute him by garrotting him with piano wire or throwing him into a gas chamber — the usual fates for captured spies.

Instead, he was allowed to march into the camp courtyard with as much strength and dignity as his torture-wracked and wounded body would allow. There he was stood up against a wall and executed by firing squad in the time-honoured fashion preferred by military personnel.

True to form, Bieler faced his executioners with the same steely reserve he had shown throughout his years as a combatant. He refused the customary blindfold.

Three days after Bieler's execution, Beekman and three other female SOE agents were marched into a yard at Dachau concentration camp near Munich. They were told to kneel by a wall. Each was killed with a single shot to the back of the neck.

Perhaps the best epitaph for Bieler and his doomed fellow saboteurs was something he once said to his Maissoneuve comrade, Chartrand: "Either you serve or you don't. If you do serve, you give it all you've got."

Chapter 4
The Evaders

Every instinct told Raymond LaBrosse to leave the 29 downed airmen to their own devices and make his escape before the Gestapo picked him up. Operation Oaktree had been blown sky-high. Its leader was in prison and many of its Resistance fighters rounded up.

If caught, the worst the others faced, as legitimate aircrew, was a German prisoner of war camp. LaBrosse would undoubtedly be tortured and executed as a spy. Espionage agents were not protected under the Geneva Convention. Numerous horror stories had already filtered back to the Allies about the ruthless and inhumane way the Nazis treated saboteurs and secret agents who fell into their clutches.

It wouldn't matter that LaBrosse had started out the war as a sergeant in the Canadian Corps of Signals. The fact remained that he had parachuted into Occupied France as an undercover agent with the British MI9 espionage unit to set up a Brittany-to-Dartmouth escape network for downed fliers and escaped Allied POWs. Call it what you might — in his present circumstances, he was a spy. His capture would undoubtedly lead to a horrible death in some vermin-infested prison cell after weeks, and perhaps months, of torture.

But there was a job to be done. Oaktree's Chief of Operations, Val Williams, was to blame for the screw-up by bragging all over France about what was supposed to be a secret operation. LaBrosse still felt obligated to make the best of a bad situation.

Williams, with two American and two Polish air-men in his charge, was captured on a train near Pau on June 4, 1943, after doing everything but install a neon sign over his head, advertising himself as an undercover agent. Within eight days, most of the Oaktree members were rounded up. LaBrosse and his band of fugitives avoided capture, but he knew the Gestapo was aware of his presence and would soon track him down.

Still he refused to abandon the men who were relying on him to get them safely back into Allied hands. Using every trick learned at espionage school, LaBrosse managed to cross most of France with 29 evaders and escapers in tow. This feat was somewhat the equivalent of making an elephant disappear into thin air.

Luckily for all of them, LaBrosse could call on a number of valuable connections in the Underground movement. These contacts were the result of a parachute jump into France near the Forest of Rambouillet on the outskirts of Paris on February 28, 1943. The Resistance fighters helped him move his ragtag band of evacuees across German-occupied territory. It was an area teeming with collaborators looking to curry favour with their Nazi masters.

Jinxed From The Start

The mission hadn't felt right from the outset. LaBrosse had certainly been keen to take on the assignment after a British Intelligence major had asked him all sorts of strange questions during a London interview in August 1942. Did he like sports? Adventure? As a boy, what games had he most enjoyed? How did he feel about the war? About the Americans? The British? The French? Would he be willing to risk torture and an ignominious death behind enemy lines?

LaBrosse, a native of Ottawa who spoke fluent French and, better still, knew how to operate a wireless radio when such skills were in short supply, was told he was an ideal candidate for the job. His record described him as mature, enthusiastic, strong, and imaginative.

British Intelligence was keen on getting an escape network set up where Allied fugitives would be passed along through French Underground channels to the coast of Brittany. Once a dozen or more of these "packages" were collected, a signal would be sent to England and arrangements made for a Royal Navy motor gunboat to speed across the English Channel to pick them up. If nothing went wrong, the evacuees would be back in England within a couple of hours.

Because they were in a hurry to get the two agents in place to head up the Oaktree network, MI9 rushed LaBrosse through espionage training, including the art of parachuting. But the young Ottawa native had a natural gift for the spy game and he rose to the challenge.

His only disappointment came when he read the headlines in London papers about the Canadians landing at Dieppe. He figured all the hard knocks preparing him for his jump into Occupied France were for nothing. The war would soon be over.

It wasn't long though before Dieppe was revealed as a fiasco. LaBrosse's clandestine operation would be going ahead after all. Then his up-and-down emotions took another dip when little things started to go wrong.

A Russian/American Partner

The first warning signal came during his initial meeting with fellow agent Williams. Born Vladimir Bouryschkine in Moscow in 1913, Williams had emigrated with his family from revolutionary Russia — first to France, then to the United States. Back in France in 1940 as a volunteer with the American Red Cross, he helped Albert-Marie Guerisse, a Belgian posing as "Pat O'Leary", spirit escapers and evaders from Marseilles to Gibraltar on their way to London.

LaBrosse would later say that Williams was the worst type of individual for the job as head of a spy network. "Whereas he was very courageous, from the security point of view he was extremely careless and lived on expediencies. He was hopeless from the point of view of security, just hopeless."

Fate also seemed to send up warning signals when the Halifax bomber, from which they would parachute into occupied territory, kept having trouble locating the assigned drop zone. Nine nights in a row, the two men went through the nerve-wracking preparations for their assignment. Nine times they risked being shot down over the English Channel or Occupied France. Nine times the bomber had to return its human cargo to the Tempsford Royal Air Force (RAF) station.

The frustrations of the aborted missions seemed to bring out the hedonist in Williams. To alleviate the boredom of sitting around waiting for the next aircraft to take off, the agent insisted on making tours of the local pubs. There, he complained long and loud about what he saw as the inefficiency of the RAF in getting him and his fellow agent into Occupied France.

This complete breach of security — not to mention the traitorous remarks he was making about the military during wartime — should have landed him in prison. In fact, it nearly did. But MI9 was desperate to set up the escape route and had invested too much time and effort in Williams to see him spend the duration of the war in Wormwood Scrubs. They managed to smooth the ruffled feathers of the RAF top brass and Williams was left to foul things up much later on, when the damage would be far worse.

When the two agents finally landed in France on their tenth run, LaBrosse checked his wireless radio and found it badly damaged from the jump. Reluctantly, he used a Free French intelligence group to wire London, asking for new equipment. He knew it was risky to use operatives unknown to him, but there was no other choice.

The Evaders

British Intelligence arranged to have a new radio smuggled into France from Spain. Once again, LaBrosse put his life on the line. He picked up the package at the left luggage office at the Bordeaux railway station.

Oaktree Aborted

When the second wireless proved faulty, British Intelligence scrapped Operation Oaktree's first and, as it turned out, only rescue attempt. They decided that without adequate communications equipment for last-minute arrangements, they could not take a chance on sending Royal Navy gunboats to Brittany to pick up the 86 airmen hiding in and around the Château de Bourblanc on the French coast.

With Williams arrested, the Gestapo captured a number of the downed fliers along with the Château's owners, Count and Countess de Mauduit (she was an American). This prompted LaBrosse to set out for Southern France with his 29 fugitive airmen. Reaching Toulouse, he made the dangerous trek across the Pyrénées Mountains via Andorra into Spain. From there, the group sailed by ship to Gibraltar, then on to London, and safety.

For LaBrosse, it should have meant the end of his espionage days. The Gestapo knew him by reputation and they would be looking for him should he show up

73

again in Occupied France. British Intelligence, under normal circumstance, would insist on keeping returned agents from heading back into a situation threatening almost certain capture.

But these weren't normal circumstances. More and more Allied aircraft were being shot down over Northern France in the rush to soften up the area for the upcoming Invasion. The need for an escape route from Brittany, across the English Channel, was becoming crucial. LaBrosse wouldn't rest until he convinced his superiors that he was the man for the job.

Ken Woodhouse

Ken Woodhouse was undergoing what felt like an out-of-body experience. It was as though he was witnessing his own capture by German soldiers. He was several thousand feet above the French countryside, somewhere south of Amiens, descending serenely to earth in his parachute harness. But what he saw below was anything but bucolic.

His abandoned Spitfire screamed towards a wooded area near the village of Remerangles. Looking west, he saw a small truck kicking up dust as it raced for the spot where he would land. No doubt, it was loaded with German troops ready to capture him, or even shoot him, if they were in a vengeful mood. The odds were that one or more of them would have lost family or friends in an Allied bombing raid.

"They sure don't give a guy much of a head start," Woodhouse later remembered thinking. It was a pity they were on to him because as a former denizen of the Canadian Prairies, he might have given them the slip somewhere in the miles of rolling farmland he could see from his vantage point. Still, if he could land a few minutes before they caught up with him, he might be able to hide his parachute, race for that wooded area below, and hide out until nightfall.

A loud thud interrupted his thoughts. He looked toward the direction of the noise. His Spitfire was ploughing into the dense woods. Woodhouse and his fellow pilots in 401 Squadron were victims of deadly air locks that shut down the plane's engines when a switch was made from auxiliary fuel tanks to the main system. With his Spitfire bucking and heaving like a bronco in distress, Woodhouse had aimed the aircraft southward, hoping to make at least a few more kilometres before the engine died completely.

The advice given pilots, if their single-engine fighters had to be abandoned over Occupied France, was to fly them as far south as they could get before bailing out. If they turned north and tried to make it back to their base in England, they might end up drowning in the

English Channel or jumping into the militarized zone along the French coast, heavily fortified by armed-to-the-teeth German troops expecting an Allied invasion.

Southern France Safer

The southern part of France, under the Vichy Government led by Field Marshall Pétain, was a safer bet. Much of the population was sympathetic to the Allied cause and would help downed airmen escape into Spain.

With the Spitfire engine showing no intention of re-starting, Woodhouse had realized he was about as far south as he was going to get. He had quickly pulled back the glass canopy of the doomed aircraft and tumbled out into the wild blue yonder.

Woodhouse hit the ground heavily, injuring his left knee. He struggled to gather in the silk folds of his parachute, hoping at least to hide any evidence of his landing. But he was just going through the exercise. He knew it would be a matter of seconds before the Germans arrived.

To his surprise, there was only one man in the small panel truck that pulled up about 100 metres away from him. Not only did the driver appear too old for military service, he was dressed in the blue smock and trousers of a French farmer, not the military grey of a German soldier. He looked threatening as he waved his hands and arms about wildly and shouted at Woodhouse in French, a language a boy from the Prairies didn't understand.

Gesticulating towards a pile of hay in the back of the truck, the man seemed to want Woodhouse to bury himself in it, along with his parachute. Hardly the actions of an enemy soldier, but could he be a collaborator?

Woodhouse decided to trust him and that decision barely saved him from being taken captive. Within seconds of his burying himself under the hay and the truck starting up, Woodhouse felt the vehicle come to an abrupt stop and heard a heated exchange between the driver and someone outside the cab. Woodhouse didn't speak German either but he had seen enough newsreels of a ranting Adolf Hitler to recognize the guttural German being fired at the driver.

His rescuer somehow managed to send the German patrol on a wild goose chase. Woodhouse was told later that when asked if he had seen a parachute descending, the truck driver pointed to the area near the crashed Spitfire.

Taking Evasive Action
The Frenchman took his guest back to his farm where he was put up in hay shed until arrangements could be made to get him to safety. Woodhouse immediately set

about extracting a sharp knife he carried in one of his flying boots. He used it to cut the tops of the boots off to make them look like ordinary shoes. He then took a razor blade from his escape kit — standard issue to all Allied aircrew — and sliced the pilot wings from his battle dress jacket, hiding them in his "new" shoes in case he had to convince a captor that he was a downed flier and not a spy. He taped his identity tags onto the back of one leg and pocketed his expensive Rolex watch, a gift from his parents. The average Frenchman would not be sporting a Rolex and Woodhouse anticipated he would soon be playing the role of an average Frenchman.

Woodhouse's rescuer reappeared with his wife and son and handed the pilot a loaf of bread and a bottle of cider. Now somewhat calmer than he had been just after the parachute landing, the farmer was able to communicate in broken English he had picked up from other downed airmen. He identified himself as Maurice Rendu, a member of the French Underground for years. He told Woodhouse he would be back for him at dusk.

That evening, Woodhouse was loaded back into the small truck and taken to Rendu's parents' house in a nearby village where he was introduced to two rough-looking characters in French work clothes. They turned out to be the remnants of an American bomber crew. Also present was a member of the French Resistance, who spoke perfect English and began peppering the three airmen with questions about life in North America.

Woodhouse flunked miserably when it came to baseball. As a Western Canadian, he was a hockey fan. But his scorecard must have chalked up more rights than wrongs because his interrogator seemed to believe he was legitimate.

Two days later, all three men were herded back into the truck, with Rendu's father Wilfred driving and the chief of the police of the area — a long-time member of the *maquis* movement of the French Resistance — riding shotgun. Along the way to their destination, a large town where the chances of capture wouldn't be so great, they picked up four more airmen — one of whom was an American tailgunner, shot up before bailing out, his wounds attended by a sympathetic French surgeon.

Arriving at their destination, the seven men were turned over to other members of the French Resistance, provided with identity cards and train tickets, and then eventually put on a train for Paris under the care of new handlers. These escorts were appalled when they inspected the fugitives' ID cards, declaring them so badly made that it would be better if they had no papers at all. As Woodhouse watched in horror, the identity cards were ripped to pieces and the bits of paper scattered out the train window.

Stupid Blunder

Arriving at the Paris Gare du Nord without incident, Woodhouse and his fellow evaders cringed and stopped dead in their tracks as they walked toward the exit. The wounded American air gunner fell behind in the crush of people leaving the train and unwittingly yelled at his companions in English: "Hey, fellas, wait for me!" Miraculously in the din of voices echoing off the walls of the cavernous station, no one picked up on this senseless breach of security.

The next tense moment came when a German troop train pulled into the station and hundreds of Nazi soldiers began disembarking. This proved to be a blessing in disguise. The tide of humanity now swelled to such an extent, the airmen were carried through the gate, along with the crowd of pushing and shoving French nationals and German soldiers. While checking papers, a Gestapo agent gave up in disgust, as he was bumped and jostled by one exiting passenger after another.

Once outside the station, the fugitives were told to split up to look less conspicuous. Woodhouse and a U.S. airman were approached by an elderly couple who motioned them to follow. They were taken to the couples' apartment where they were given food. But their hosts appeared nervous, as if expecting the Gestapo to pound on their door at any moment. They were visibly relieved when a light tap on the door revealed a young woman calling for one of the fugitives. Someone would be along shortly to collect the other one.

The young woman took Woodhouse to her apartment across from the Luxembourg Gardens. This required transportation on the Métro — the Parisian subway system — and Woodhouse's heart took another hammering. Just down the car were a dozen or so drunken German soldiers who were roughing up passengers and shoving them out of seats to make room for themselves. The Canadian pilot gritted his teeth and tried not to make eye contact. Luckily, his Métro stop arrived before any curious German came over to demand his seat — or check his papers.

For the next few days, Woodhouse hid at several safe houses, as a precaution against the prying eyes of collaborators, who paid particular attention to strangers staying at one address for any length of time. He eventually ended up at Lycée St. Louis, a French high school in the heart of Paris and the apartment home of a French couple who were harbouring two other Canadian airmen.

Once again, Woodhouse felt he was being checked out as a possible German plant. The Frenchman told him he once lived in Medicine Hat, Alberta, close to the

Woodhouse family home in Prince Albert, Saskatchewan where his wife had a sister. Woodhouse didn't believe him. The two communities were more than 500 kilometres apart. The descriptions the couple gave of life in Canada sounded like they were from a book. Woodhouse told them he doubted the entire story. That ended the questioning and the tension in the air.

Better Papers Provided

Woodhouse was given new identification papers that were more authentic looking than the ones from his earlier escorts. He was also given a train ticket to St. Brieuc in Brittany, and another that would take him to a small coastal village a few kilometres farther along. Since the village was inside the 15-kilometre restricted zone that stretched along the northern coast of France, he also received a counterfeit special pass that would allow him to enter the area safely — provided the pass looked real enough to fool anyone inspecting it.

Woodhouse set off with a new guide for the railway station and was soon stopped by two French gendarmes. One of the policemen said something to Woodhouse in French. Taking a chance, he handed the man his identification papers, wondering if the ink had yet dried. After a cursory inspection, the Frenchman returned the papers and motioned Woodhouse and his guide to move along.

On rubbery legs, Woodhouse walked away from the two policemen, turned a corner, then competed in a two-man race with his guide for several blocks as they tried to put as much distance as they could between themselves and the inquisitive gendarmes. Reaching a café where the guide knew the owner, the two men were given a stiff drink to calm their nerves.

The moment arrived when Woodhouse was sure the jig was up. Reaching the station, he was turned over to another escort, this one a feisty young Frenchwoman who didn't suffer fools gladly. With seven fugitives in tow, the woman made her way through the crowded train to the compartment assigned to her and her charges. To her consternation, it was crammed with French passengers who refused to budge. Hurling insults at the squatters, the woman trooped the seven foreigners back off the train, found an official she brow-beat into accompanying them to the compartment to sort out the situation, and started the whole process all over again.

Woodhouse expected someone to step into the fray at any moment and begin grilling the group about who they were and why they were making such a fuss. But after the railway official kicked the interlopers out of the compartment, the only result was surly stares from the other passengers. The guide suggested they thought

Woodhouse and his companions were important German officials pulling rank to remove legitimate passengers from their seats.

At dawn, the train arrived at St. Brieuc station and the seven fugitives walked the gauntlet of angry glares as they left the coach. A tram provided the short ride to the coast, with standing room only. Rubbing shoulders with German soldiers, Woodhouse spent several hours avoiding eye contact for fear one of the Germans would engage him in conversation.

Entering The Restricted Zone

The tram eventually arrived at Guingamp, the entry point to the restricted zone. Woodhouse and his companions braced themselves for a grilling as they passed through the station gate. Dressed in civilian clothes and carrying false identification papers, they would undoubtedly be shot as spies if they were caught.

Even worse, they now possessed knowledge about escape routes, the names of French patriots who had helped them and places they had stayed. Being shot trying to flee would be far better than being arrested and tortured for information.

To their surprise and relief, no one stopped them or even asked for their papers as they walked out onto the station platform. Once again, they split up and

The Evaders

Woodhouse found himself and one of the other fugitives turned over to the care of yet another nervous couple. He surmised that since no one had checked his papers at the station, his benefactors might be worried that he and his fellow travellers were under surveillance as decoys to flush out locals who were part of the escape network.

After being passed on to another guide, Woodhouse and his companion were taken to a large house nearby, owned by a woman who gave them soap and water and a bed for the night. She spoke reasonable English and during a short conversation with her, Woodhouse learned she had sheltered at least two dozen Allied airmen in the past couple of years.

Late the next day, Woodhouse and his companion were taken to a truck and told to crowd in with six other fugitives who were already aboard. After a brief and uncomfortable journey, Woodhouse and two others were offloaded and led away by a young girl who took them to a farmhand's cabin. There they spent the night.

The next morning, the same youngster led them along a wooded trail, picking up other fugitives along the way. Without warning, the group stumbled onto a German army post. Some of the evacuees dived into the bushes along the edge of the trail. Woodhouse and several others, caught flat-footed in the open, decided to

85

bluff their way through. They were dressed as French civilians and there were hundreds, if not thousands, of transients wandering the French countryside at the time.

Germans Really Russians
Their ruse worked and they shuffled by the disinterested Germans without incident. Only after they were safely back in the woods did they learn from their young guide that the "Germans" weren't more attentive because they were actually White Russians captured on the Eastern Front and forced to fight for Germany.

Woodhouse and his group eventually reached their destination at Plouha on a cliff above the English Channel. At a signal received over the BBC (British Broadcasting Corporation) World Service, the Canadian Spitfire pilot and a number of other Allied airmen were herded down the cliff by two tough looking individuals who seemed to be in charge of the operation. One was in his late thirties, a short, stocky man with dark hair and a moustache. The other was a young 4man in his mid-20s, a bit taller, with a square jaw and quiet demeanour. Both spoke French with an accent different from those heard by Woodhouse so far on his flight to freedom.

The next few hours were a blur of activity. Two rubber boats with muffled oars, each craft manned by two Royal Navy sailors, appeared out of the darkness and the fugitives were rowed out to Motor Gunboat 503. At full throttle, the vessel raced back to England and freedom for Woodhouse and his companions.

On March 26, 1944, the downed pilot walked into the Dispersal Hut at the Biggins Hill air base of 401 Squadron in England. There was a moment of stunned silence, then a shout of recognition, mixed with disbelief. Ken "Woody" Woodhouse, shot down over Occupied France, was back with his squadron in less than 10 days. And what stories he had to tell.

Chapter 5
The Shelburn Line

Ken Woodhouse had no way of knowing who they were because they spoke in short bursts of French, and only when necessary. As it happened, the two guardian angels who helped him into a Royal Navy dinghy at Plouha on his way back to England were fellow Canadians Lucien Dumais and Raymond LaBrosse. No one — not even their closest confidantes running the escape route — knew their true identity. That way, if the Gestapo rounded up any of them and submitted them to torture, there would be minimal danger of the network being compromised and the leaders arrested.

The Shelburn Line

As the launch date for the Normandy Invasion approached, General Dwight D. Eisenhower and Allied Command greatly escalated the number of bombing missions into Northern France to destroy port installations, factories, roads, rail lines, and other strategic sites. Their objective was to soften up German defences to make the D-Day landings much easier and keep the loss of Allied invaders to a minimum.

Inevitably, more bombing missions meant more flight crews bailing out of crippled aircraft. It became imperative to set up an escape route on the northern coast of France, rather than traipsing the airmen down the entire length of France and over the Pyrénées to Spain. After many reconnaissance patrols by British Intelligence agents and their counterparts in the *maquis*, the village of Plouha in Brittany was picked as the ideal mustering area for the "packages", the code-name for the fugitive Allies. An earlier escape via the Normandy coast by Gabriel Chartrand and three other eluders proved a rescue operation from Northern France could be carried out effectively.

The Shelburn Line was the name given to the network of Allied agents and French Resistance fighters who would form the human chain that would pass escapers and evaders along until they were salted away in farmhouses around Plouha awaiting rescue.

Operation Bonaparte was the code word for the actual rescue exercise, named for the beach from which the fugitives would depart.

Dumais and LaBrosse shared the same resolve to make the escape network a success, but had different reasons for agreeing to risk their lives to set it up.

Dumais' Volatility

Dumais admitted to a short fuse and a bad temper. He still bristled at the memory of having to surrender at Dieppe. His blood boiled whenever images flared up in his mind of him and his fellow Canadian soldiers being treated like cattle as they were herded onto a train for transport to a German prisoner-of-war camp.

Back in England after his daring escape from a German prison train and a Resistance-assisted trek down through the middle of France, he had been approached by MI9. That section of British Intelligence, directly responsible for setting up escape networks in enemy-occupied territory, wanted him to go back into Occupied France as a spy.

Dumais had considered himself a professional soldier ever since joining the reserves as a 29-year-old in 1934. After pondering MI9's request, he felt the best way to extract revenge against the Nazis for the deaths and humiliation of his Dieppe comrades would be by returning to active duty. He spent four months with the British First Army in North Africa, sometimes on horseback behind enemy lines doing reconnaissance work.

Following his service with the British First Army, Dumais returned to his old unit, Les Fusiliers Mont-Royal, in mid-1943, but after his adventures at Dieppe, his adrenaline-churning escape from the Germans and the excitement of North Africa, the day-to-day drudgery of camp life bored him.

Furthermore, he couldn't stop thinking of others, like himself, who were alone in enemy territory, desperate for help in avoiding capture and fearing the consequences that would surely follow their incarceration in a Nazi prison.

He also had to acknowledge his bad temper played a direct part in his decision to head back into enemy territory. After several run-ins with his regimental commanding officer, a man for whom he had little respect, MI9 got a call. They enthusiastically welcomed him into the fold.

LaBrosse More Even Tempered

LaBrosse was far more easy-going than Dumais — a characteristic that balanced his partner's more bombastic temperament and helped make them a good team. His sensitive nature left him awash in guilt for the failure of Operation Oaktree, the earlier attempt to set up an escape network from Plouha across the English Channel to Dartmouth.

Never mind that the expedition was scrubbed due to bad luck, bad weather, and bad leadership on the part of Val Williams. Ignore the fact that LaBrosse had successfully pulled off the almost-impossible feat of spiriting a bewildered band of 29 Allied airmen across France and the Pyrénées to freedom. He still burned with a desire to get that escape route established and leapt at the chance to go back when the offer was made.

LaBrosse was introduced to Dumais over lunch in a London restaurant just a few short weeks after LaBrosse's heroic escape from France. After the usual thrust and parry of initial table conversation, they hit it off.

Dumais was the older of the two by more than a dozen years, and as a sergeant-major in his old regiment, he outranked LaBrosse, a former sergeant with the Canadian Corps of Signals. There were no ranks in the escape network, but Dumais' seniority in age and military experience made him the logical choice as leader. LaBrosse, who had hoped to run his own show, was impressed with his new comrade and readily agreed to the arrangement.

To be certain they would make an efficient team, the two men were ordered to spend a week together in

London, living in the same room, sizing each other up. When this living out of each other's pockets went off without a hitch, they were sent for training to refresh their skills as operators in enemy territory. They were given the latest gadgets to help them carry out their roles — fountain pens that fired a deadly gas, buttons that hid compasses. They were also provided with large amounts of French francs and fake identity papers.

But the team's return to France wasn't to be without incident. After completing their refresher course, the two men climbed into the cramped confines of a tiny Lysander aircraft to be flown across the English Channel for a pre-arranged landing where they would be met by a French Resistance unit.

As they reached the French coast, their light and slow-moving plane was buffeted by cannon fire from a German night fighter that had chanced upon them. They were forced to take evasive action as the pilot turned the aircraft around for an emergency return to England.

The German aircraft made several passes at them, but their slowness actually worked to their advantage. The enemy plane almost stalled in its attempt to slow down enough to draw a bead on the Lysander. The German pilot eventually gave up in frustration, flying off to find a bigger, richer prize.

A second attempt on a rainy night, ten days later, also had to be abandoned. The pilot of another Lysander radioed that his aircraft was bogged down in French mud. It would be foolhardy to try to land another plane.

Turning back for England, the plane carrying Dumais and LaBrosse was shelled by anti-aircraft fire over the French coast. The pilot opened up the aircraft's engine for all it was worth, and its occupants were soon back on British soil. They heard the next day from base personnel that a farmer with a team of horses had managed to pull the bogged-down Lysander out of the mud just before daylight. It limped home to England on its last drops of fuel.

One More Try
Dumais and LaBrosse had twice gone through the exercise of taking off for France and narrowly escaped being shot down on both occasions. They began to feel there was a jinx on the Lysanders and suggested they should be allowed to parachute in. This operation had its own risks. Their MI9 control agent told them they would give the Lysanders one more try before going the parachute route.

Finally, on their third run, the pilot of the small aircraft spotted signal fires on the ground in the rendezvous area. He brought the Lysander in without incident and the two agents were once again on enemy soil. It was here that Dumais learned there were nerves of steel under LaBrosse's calm exterior.

When you land in Occupied territory, you put your life in the hands of local freedom fighters who must trust you as well. You don't want to do anything to sour the relationship. Everyone's nerves are on edge, and it is an effort to keep everyone cordial.

The two agents weren't in France for more than a few minutes when an incident occurred that had everyone sucking in their breath in anticipation of what would happen next.

As the French Resistance fighters welcomed the two newcomers, everyone started grabbing up the offloaded equipment in an attempt to get away from the rendezvous area as quickly as possible. LaBrosse's suitcase, containing his wireless radio — the agents' lifeline to London — was between his feet. One of the Frenchmen reached for it to carry it away.

"*Laissez ça tranquille!*" LaBrosse hissed through clenched teeth. "Leave it alone!"

There was tension in the air as the two men eyed each other. Then the Frenchman gave a small smile and a classic Gallic shrug and reached for another piece of equipment. The moment passed without incident, but

Dumais noticed his comrade was afforded a substantial amount of respect from then on.

The two Canadians, having arrived safely in France, began recruiting local assistance and arranging lodging in the Brittany countryside for the numerous "packages" needing assistance in getting safely back to England. After many trials and tribulations, Operation Bonaparte and the Shelburn Escape and Evasion Line were now a reality.

Straightforward Operation

In theory, the exercise was relatively simple. Members of the French Resistance would funnel the Allied fugitives through various routes of the Shelburn Line to the Plouha area on the Brittany coast. They would be secreted in farmhouses until a dozen or more were on hand. LaBrosse would then signal London in meticulously prepared code, indicating that an evacuation was in order. He, Dumais, and their top aides would then gather in their stone farmhouse headquarters, known as The House of Alphonse, where they would listen to the BBC French radio network.

This was a service that repeated a steady stream of short messages, supposedly for the families of an estimated 120,000 Free French soldiers who had escaped to England after their units, along with the British

Expedition Force, were decimated by the advancing
Germans in May 1940. In total, a flotilla of British naval
vessels and small private craft answering the call for volunteers, rescued some 340,000 British and French soldiers from the beaches of Dunkirk.

The BBC French radio network was also used
extensively by British Intelligence to send coded messages to their operatives in Occupied France. Pre-
arranged phrases, that made no sense to German military eavesdroppers, would indicate an upcoming event,
such as the imminent arrival of a Royal Navy Motor Gun
Boat (MGB) off the Brittany coast.

When the words: *Bonjour, tout le monde à la mai-
son d'Alphonse* were broadcast, this meant the British
vessel would set off under cover of darkness for its dash
across the English Channel. A different coded message
would mean the trip was called off for security reasons.
A third French phrase indicated the MGB had, in fact,
left Dartmouth and would arrive shortly.

The "packages" received a final briefing, including
a warning the last mile to freedom would be the most
treacherous of their entire escapade. Not only was the
hill down to the beach catacombed with mines, but fre-
quent German patrols would hear even the smallest
pebble dislodged on the descent.

Should one of the evacuees ask why the mines

weren't simply removed, it was explained that the success of the entire operation hinged on the Germans not being aware the escape network existed. If the mines were dug up and hauled off somewhere to be detonated — or used against the Germans by saboteurs — it would be a dead give-away that clandestine activities were being carried out right under the Germans' noses.

Being an efficient lot, the Germans would change the locations of the mines from time to time. It was the job of one of the one brave French Resistance fighters to keep a close watch on the minefield through binoculars and note the spots where the explosives were relocated. Then he would inch down the hill shortly before a rescue operation and put a small piece of white cloth beside each mine.

By keeping a sharp eye out for these markers, the evacuation party could negotiate the hill in safety. Once the "packages" were on their way, the bits of cloth would be removed until the next rescue operation.

While the evacuation exercise was straightforward enough, it was impossible to gain control of two variables — the weather and human nature. Gales that lasted for weeks and blundering idiots who didn't think before acting or speaking would hamper the operation on several occasions.

Dumais and LaBrosse landed back in France on

November 19, 1943 and immediately set about getting
the evacuation network in place. They were elated at the
number of French locals who were willing to hide evacuees, lead them to safe houses in the Plouha area, or
look after the many other little details that such an operation required.

There were interpreters to help the English-
speaking fugitives and their French-speaking rescuers
communicate. Physicians were recruited to treat the
sick or wounded. A quartermaster was selected to take
on the onerous task of finding food and clothing for the
evacuees in a time of scarcity and rationing. Printers
were located who were willing to produce false identity
papers and counterfeit ration coupons on short notice.

First Evacuation Planned
Things went so smoothly that the first rescue mission
was set for December 15, less than a month after the two
agents had landed in France. With 16 airmen hidden in
farmhouses in and around Plouha, LaBrosse sent the
coded wireless message to British Intelligence, indicating all was in readiness.

With the receipt of the radio greeting to everybody
at the house of Alphonse, everyone made last-minute
preparations for the treacherous descent down the
hillside to the evacuation beach. Then a second coded

message came through. Gale force winds in the Channel meant that night's crossing was cancelled.

For eight more days, the Bonaparte crew and their bored, nervous charges sweated it out. Finally, a message was delivered, scrapping the exercise until further notice — and better weather.

That's when human nature surfaced to make a bad situation worse. Disappointment at having the rescue mission scrubbed and frustration at being cooped up with French families who spoke little or no English caused the fugitives to become restive. Some would try to persuade their local helpers to take them to the nearest pub or café — anywhere that would break the monotony.

These pleas were refused because of the risks involved — causing more surliness and tense feelings. It was a struggle to keep some of the younger, brasher aircrew members from sneaking out and heading for the relatively bright lights of downtown Plouha.

Much to everyone's relief, the storms subsided and the tides were favourable for another rescue attempt late in January. At 6 p.m., on the evening of January 29, 1944, a rousing hello to everybody at Alphonse's house sent the 16 bored airmen and two outward-bound British agents into action. At 9 p.m., a second message was received, indicating the MGB was in the midst of a

140-kilometre dash across the Channel to Plouha.

The dangerous descent of the cliffs started at midnight, with one member of the French Resistance remaining at the top sending the Morse Code letter "B" by flashlight at one-minute intervals out into the Channel. A cardboard tube attached to the rubber-coated torch directed the beam seaward.

At about 1:15 a.m., the anxious evacuation party saw three dark shapes out on the water bobbing silently toward them. It was a Royal Navy landing party in rubber boats, each manned by two bareheaded sailors. Their caps were left back on the MGB in case they blew off as the men made their way to shore. Royal Navy headgear washing up on Bonaparte Beach would not go unnoticed by daylight German patrols.

The landing area became a tableau of carefully executed manoeuvres as arms, money, and stores were silently offloaded. The fugitives were directed by hand signals to hunker down in one of the three air-filled dinghies. With a barely audible swish of rubber on sand, the boats were back in the water, making their way to the MGB within 15 minutes of landing. In a few short hours, the 16 airmen and two British agents would be safe and sound in England.

Armed And Dangerous

The MGB speeding the evacuees to freedom was 37 metres long. Its three diesel engines were capable of great speed, even while carrying a crew of 36 and whatever number of "packages" the Shelburn Network posted. The Royal Navy craft was armed with a six-pound gun aft, a two-pound gun forward, and twin machine guns aft of the bridge.

The Dartmouth (and sometimes Helford) to Plouha runs were codenamed "Alibi". Each member of the MGB crew carried false passports and identification papers indicating they were French nationals.

As the tensions of the past hours, days, and weeks began to subside, Dumais and LaBrosse admitted to each other that, elated as they were by Operation Bonaparte's first success, their joy was tempered by exhaustion and a sense of longing. They yearned to be back in England. Instead, they trudged back up the hillside with their French cohorts to face a decidedly uncertain future.

The reappearance of LaBrosse's old boss, Val Williams, almost spelled the end of Operation Bonaparte before they could make their second evacuation at the end of February. After a spectacular escape from Rennes prison, Williams showed up in Paris where he still had a few contacts. One of them got in touch with LaBrosse, who managed to persuade a reluctant Dumais to seek permission from MI9 to include the escaped prisoner in the contingent waiting for an MGB to take them to England.

Bad Apple Returns

That act of kindness almost blew the whole operation apart, due to gross stupidity on the part of Williams — who should have known better. Hobbling on a fractured leg, he showed up at the St. Brieuc train station, leaning on the arm of a Russian officer whom he had promised to get safely to England — without advance permission from Dumais or LaBrosse. What's more, the two fugitives were roaring drunk, smoking English cigarettes, and conversing in English and Russian — in the middle of German-occupied France.

When a shocked and disgusted Dumais heard how Williams and his companion had put the whole network in peril, he was ready to execute them on the spot with the pistol he carried.

The less volatile LaBrosse pointed out that, rather than having to dispose of the two bodies and explain to MI9 what happened to their fair-haired boy, it would be easier to put the fear of God into Williams' companion and send him packing. Intense questioning of this hanger-on revealed he knew nothing about the network. He

believed a few of his new-found friend's former colleagues had offered them a free ride to England. That
would leave only Williams to deal with and MI9 had
expressed a keen interest in debriefing him about his
arrest and incarceration.

Dumais was quick to anger, but just as quick to
cool down under the calm reasoning of his fellow agent.
He decided to comply with LaBrosse's wishes. But he
insisted that a coded message be telegraphed to
England saying that if they ever again sent Williams
back to France as a spy, Dumais would shoot him on
sight.

Chapter 6
Close Calls

Dumais' threat to do away with Williams if he was ever foolish enough to show his face in the Plouha area again was not an idle one. He wouldn't be the first person posing a risk to the security of the Shelburn Line and Operation Bonaparte that Dumais and his colleagues were forced to execute to protect their organization.

One of the greatest dangers facing the escape networks was a concerted effort by the Germans to have their agents or French collaborators penetrate the individual cells operating within the umbrella group. They would do so by pretending to be French nationals sympathetic to the Allied cause or by playing the role of fugitives requiring evacuation to England.

The rationale for German infiltrators seeking to eradicate the escape networks was understandable. Every downed Allied airman returned to his unit was another enemy who would soon be back in the business of raining bombs down on Germany. It was a puzzle to some, however, why there were French men and women willing to expose Allied agents and their own countrymen to Nazi torture, and more often than not, excruciating death.

There were several rationales for this traitorous behaviour. Some French people believed it was better to live under Nazi domination than allow the communists to take over the French government, as the Fascist propaganda agents claimed to be a clear and present danger. There were others in it for greed. Cozying up to the Germans led to perks their fellow Frenchmen didn't get. Still others were motivated by threats of reprisal by the Nazis against loved ones sent to German work camps.

Whatever the reason, there were hundreds and perhaps thousands of French nationals who would turn in an Allied agent or downed airmen to the dreaded Gestapo or SS termination squads without giving it so much as a second thought.

Checks And Balances

This being the case, every would-be Resistance member and fugitive claiming to be a downed airman or escaped soldier faced interrogation to make sure they were bona fide. Too many cells were compromised and their members arrested because a collaborator or Nazi agent duped an unwary member of an escape network.

As horror stories circulated about cell members being betrayed, arrested, and brutally tortured before being executed, more and more precautions were taken to weed out the betrayers. In some cases, innocent people might well have been wrongfully executed as collaborators, but it was considered a small misfortune compared to all the lives that would be put in jeopardy if security were breached.

On one occasion, Dumais grilled a man claiming to be a Free Norwegian airman shot down in a raid. He claimed to be with the Royal Air Force and was keen on getting back to England so he could get the chance to fight the Nazis once again.

His answers were right on the money when it came to details about his squadron, the airfield where he was based, and the service personnel he came into contact with. But he became evasive, even agitated, when Dumais asked him questions about Norway. He said he hadn't been there in a long time. Suspecting a rat,

Dumais became brutal in his questioning, tripping the "Norwegian" up time and again.

Finally, the man could take it no longer. He broke down and confessed he was a Nazi agent and the information he had been giving came from questioning captured RAF aircrews. The exposed spy pleaded with Dumais and the other members of Operation Bonaparte to let him join their organization. He promised to give them valuable information about how much the Germans knew about their operations.

Dumais felt that, under the circumstances, he had every right to lead the man along, just as the would-be infiltrator had tried to do to them. The first thing determined was the Germans didn't even know there was a sophisticated escape network in place. The exercise was a fishing expedition to see what their plant could turn up. He was convinced the group was an independent Resistance unit dabbling in getting fugitives out of the country.

With every bit of valuable information squeezed out of the "Norwegian", it was felt he knew too much about the people in the group. To protect the operation, the man was taken out into the woods and shot.

However, Dumais, LaBrosse, and company would take every precaution possible to avoid killing an innocent person. There was the case of a young airman who identified himself as Robert Fruth from Ohio. While he was able to answer questions about his home state without any difficulty, he failed miserably when the interrogation turned to more recent events.

"Fruth" couldn't answer questions about his squadron, his bomb group, the names of the pilot and crew of his plane, or the target he was headed for when he was shot down. A Resistance member with an itchy trigger finger wanted to shoot the man on the spot, convinced he was a Nazi agent. But LaBrosse wanted to check the man out with England. He tapped out a wireless signal asking for details and somehow managed to keep the impulsive Frenchman contained during the long hours of waiting for a return message.

Clearance Given

As it turned out, Fruth was legit. Having just arrived in England from the United States, he was roused from bed, his very first night, to replace a gunner suddenly taken ill. It was his misfortune to be shot down on his first sortie, before he had even had a chance to learn the names of the people he was flying with. Rather than being shot, he was one of the "packages" evacuated on the next Plouha to Dartmouth run.

To avoid the execution of innocent people, flawed questions were devised that a genuine Allied fugitive would see through but a German agent might get tripped up on. For instance, an American bombardier answered all the simple stuff without any problems. He knew the movies playing on his base back in England prior to his last raid, who Betty Grable and Rita Hayworth were, and that Bugs and Porky were cartoon characters. He was able to answer questions about Huck Finn and Tom Sawyer, and knew that "Mairzy Doats" was a hit record about the feeding habits of barnyard animals.

The bombardier twigged to the trick questions right away. He knew the Pittsburgh Pirates of baseball's National League couldn't have lost any games to the Chicago Bears because the Bears were a football team. He knew Dizzy Dean never pitched for the Detroit White Sox, but for the St. Louis Cardinals and the Chicago Cubs. And besides, it was the Detroit Tigers, not the White Sox. The man earned himself a seat on the next motor gunboat out of Plouha.

It was just as important for the security of the network for the "packages" to avoid making silly mistakes while on their way to the safe houses. They were instructed not to fill their lungs with smoke but to savour each cigarette by letting it smoulder between their lips as a Frenchman would, developing a long ash. They were never to offer a cigarette to anyone else. No self-respecting Frenchman would do that. Wartime cigarettes were both scarce and expensive.

No Eye Contact

If they couldn't speak French, they were told not to make eye contact with German soldiers on a train or the Métro, in case the other party decided to strike up a conversation. Better to assume the role of an embittered Frenchman who was surly to the German intruders and refused to speak to them. A lot of French people treated the occupiers that way and the Germans had come to expect it.

In spite of precautions, a lot of stupid blunders were made. Some of them led to arrests and the betrayal of a cell. Others got by unnoticed, much to the relief — and often the incredulity — of fugitive and rescuer alike.

Like the occasion when a German soldier on a train asked an Allied airmen, disguised as a French worker, for the time by motioning to his own wrist. The fugitive instinctively stretched out his arm so the German could read the time for himself. Only then did the evader realize his blunder. He was wearing an American wristwatch. Fortunately, the German didn't notice the gaffe, nodded his thanks, and turned back to the magazine he was reading.

On another occasion, an American standing in the aisle on a crowded train put his last cigarette between his lips, crumpled the package, and tossed it to the floor. It was an American brand. An alert fellow fugitive casually, but quickly, kicked it under a seat.

Even SOE agents weren't immune. One of them confessed to a colleague that, while walking down a crowded street in Paris, he realized something was wrong. Then it dawned on him he was whistling: *It's A Long Way To Tipperary*. No wonder he was getting strange looks from the other pedestrians.

Loose Lips

Human emotions also proved dangerous — and sometimes fatal. No matter how often the fugitives were reminded not to blurt out anything in English, a sudden scare or a moment of ill humour, and they would let loose with a curse that immediately labelled them as enemy aliens. In fact, there were so many stupid errors made by the Allied evaders, their French handlers would often refer to them as "the children".

There were also a number of documented cases, where treachery on the part of a lover of a cell member, led to a betrayal of the network and the arrest of its members. Gaby Chartrand attempted to contact his superior after a narrow escape by telephoning him at his mistress's apartment. A German-accented voice picked up the phone and Chartrand quickly disengaged. The mistress must have taken up with a German officer, betraying the entire cell to the Nazis. This later proved to be the case.

A weakness for the demon rum — or more likely in these cases, wine or brandy — resulted in more than one loose-tongued agent or *maquis* member being arrested, tortured, and forced to betray his comrades. It was surprising how many people, who should have known better, would allow themselves to drink too much, then tell anyone who would listen that they were involved in a clandestine operation. There were always collaborators and squealers around ready to listen.

Still, for the number of downed Allied airmen, escaped POWs, foreign agents, and French Resistance fighters involved in the dozen or more escape lines in Western Europe, it is amazing that so many came through their own personal dangers and lived to a ripe old age.

MI9 records show the networks managed to return several hundred soldiers and an estimated 3,000 Allied airmen to England. But the price paid by civilian volunteers was high. Calculations reveal one escape line worker lost his or her life for every fighting man who was led to safety.

Many of these doomed individuals died a horrible death in Gestapo torture chambers or concentration camps. Others were shot in the streets while trying to avoid arrest. Their only marker, in many cases, is a small plaque on a building or bridge near where they fell, identifying them only as an unknown freedom fighter and adding the epitaph: *Mort pour la patrie.*

Chapter 7
The Liberation of France

Dumais and LaBrosse made regular train trips between Brittany and Paris as they oversaw the inner workings of Operation Bonaparte and the Shelburn Line. At first, these sojourns were particularly dangerous because LaBrosse had only one wireless radio and carried it with him in a specially outfitted suitcase. With the successful launch of the MGB evacuations, several additional sets were brought in, and LaBrosse no longer had the risk of some Gestapo agent or German soldier demanding he open his suitcase during a random inspection.

LaBrosse experienced several close calls where the

cumbersome radio equipment was concerned. When he and Dumais had first arrived in Paris, LaBrosse was desperate to send a message back to England, seeking further instructions. Since the radio equipment required a fairly large open space in which to string up its lengthy aerial wire, LaBrosse took a chance and revealed his true identity to the stationmaster at the Gare Lachapelle. The man turned chalk white and told LaBrosse that approaching any of the workers in the railway station would mean being turned over to the Gestapo. While the stationmaster, a man named Doré, was a member of the French Underground, his staff were all collaborators with the Nazis.

Since it was prudent to move his transmitting from place to place to avoid detection, LaBrosse made use of the stationmaster's office on several occasions when Operation Bonaparte business took him to Paris. Doré's hospitality was only part of the reason for the visits. The stationmaster's teenaged daughter was very attractive and always seemed to make a point of being around when LaBrosse visited. Soon, the two young people were deeply in love.

Allies Invade Normandy
When the Allied Invasion of Normandy occurred on June 6, 1944, Dumais and LaBrosse were in Paris setting

the stage for yet another evacuation of Allied fugitives. Dumais, who heard the news on the radio while he was shaving, quickly towelled the lather from his face and delivered a joyful message to LaBrosse. The radio operator immediately contacted England for instructions. He and Dumais were ordered to get to Brittany as quickly as they could and stay there until further orders could be transmitted.

While Dumais was making travel arrangements, LaBrosse had one stop to make — the Gare Lachapelle. Nervously, he told the stationmaster's daughter that he was off on a dangerous mission and didn't know when, or if, he would return. Removing a ring with a huge blue stone from his finger, he presented it to Mademoiselle Doré and asked if she would marry him if he survived the war. Wiping away tears reflecting both her joy at his proposal and the sadness of knowing she might never see him again, she nodded her assent.

LaBrosse's elation was tempered, somewhat, by the revelation that the only transportation Dumais could arrange for the 400 kilometre trip to Brittany was two rather worse-for-wear bicycles. The Allied bombing in Northern France had destroyed so much of the rail infrastructure, train travel was restricted to military personnel and high-ranking civilian officials.

The two men set off from Paris early on the

morning of June 11. Although Brittany was northwest of the capital, they couldn't take the most direct route by heading straight north to the coast and then west to St. Brieuc. Just over 200 kilometres north of Paris were the Normandy Beaches where the Allies had landed less than a week before. Fierce battles were still raging and the two men would have been in grave danger even driving a tank, let alone pedalling bicycles.

Instead, Dumais and LaBrosse decided the smart thing to do was take the long way around by heading west and slightly south. The roads in that direction were still in relatively good repair and most of the German forces were attempting to stem the tide of Allied troops storming ashore in Normandy. The two agents figured that once they got due south of St. Brieuc, they could begin the northward portion of their journey. At first they found it tough going. During the evacuation exercises, long periods of idleness were punctuated by brief spurts of intense physical activity. Many days consisted of riding trains between Brittany and Paris. Others involved little more than whiling away the hours in cafes, waiting to make contact with agents. After a few hours of pedalling their bikes, the two men realized how out of shape they had become.

Painful Beginning

Still, these were not ordinary men. Determination kept their legs churning when every muscle, from calf to thigh, was screaming in protest. Before too many hours passed, the stamina they relied upon in basic training returned and they clipped off the kilometres as though they were serious contenders in the *Tour de France*.

Then, too, they would get great bursts of adrenaline when a rogue Allied fighter plane, looking for easy targets, would scream over the horizon. Some of the young pilots were trigger-happy, having experienced the thrill of battle. They would strafe anything that moved — including civilians on bicycles. At those times, the only recourse was to dive into the nearest ditch, then get up, curse, dust yourself off, and pedal furiously until the next aircraft roared into view.

Despite these interruptions and muscles that protested with each turn of the wheel, Dumais and LaBrosse knocked off about 50 kilometres by noon. Their route led them through countryside littered with shattered locomotives and splintered boxcars piled up on twisted rails, the result of Allied bombing in the weeks leading up to the Normandy Invasion.

The two men stopped for lunch in a small village where, to their delight, they found a bakery selling fresh, hot bread and a grocery that still had a small supply of food and wine. With a little imagination, their picnic by the roadside was just like a Sunday in the Bois de Boulogne. But they found it to be sheer agony to climb aboard their bicycles and begin pedalling again.

Late in the afternoon, Dumais and LaBrosse reached Chartres, about 100 kilometres southwest of Paris. There they had another surprise in store when the landlady of the boarding house they settled into for the night revealed she was originally from Québec. She proved to be quite loquacious and regaled the two men over dinner with tales about the strange ways of the New World across the Atlantic, not knowing their true identity.

The two agents managed to contain themselves and carried off their ruse of being Frenchmen heading to Brittany on urgent business — Dumais a mortician and LaBrosse a salesman of electrical medical equipment. They never batted an eye when their hostess mentioned the Dieppe Raid and the fact that British Intelligence agents were roaming the countryside ready to kill anyone who got in their way.

Setting off again the next morning after a good night's sleep, Dumais and LaBrosse were surprised to hear the unmistakable sound of bombs exploding in the distance. Coming to a long hill, they dismounted to walk their bicycles just as three P-38 Lightning aircraft zoomed overhead. The twin-fuselage aircraft were zero-ing in on a railway station down in the valley where two freight trains had pulled into a siding after the first few bombs served as a warning that more havoc was to come. The train crews were scrambling to get clear and the Lightning pilots, seeming to want to give them time to do so, made a long shallow turn before hurtling in for the attack.

The Lightnings, nicknamed *der Gabelschwanz Teufel* — the Fork-Tailed Devil — by the Germans who had fallen victim to their speed and manoeuvrability, swooped in on the abandoned trains and machine-gunned them. The pilots then turned their guns on the station. On their second run, the aircraft dropped the rest of their bombs and flew off, leaving the area in a shambles.

As Dumais and LaBrosse continued their epic journey, they came across other scenes of mass destruction. Here was a burned-out German truck; there was a crater littered with jagged pieces of an ammunition carrier. Scattered around were the bodies of bare-footed German soldiers. Their boots had been removed by enterprising villagers. These would end up on the black market in exchange for food or cigarettes.

Getting used to the mayhem around them, Dumais and LaBrosse elected to become part of the action.

When they found Allied bombers attacking a bridge they needed to cross, they actually waited, then pedalled frantically over it between salvos.

The Bicycle Thief

After just a couple of days, the two cyclists were within 120 kilometres of St. Brieuc and hoped to get there by dusk. But a German army sergeant had other plans.

As Dumais and LaBrosse, travelling with false ID in the names of Jean-François Guillou and Marcel Desjardins respectively, crossed a bridge over a small stream, a German soldier, armed with a rifle, stepped into the road and signalled them to stop. LaBrosse cursed himself for having decided back in Paris to take the radio with him as a backup rather than destroying it. It was in the suitcase on the back of his bicycle and its discovery would surely mean arrest, torture, and certain death for him and his colleague.

Dumais' thoughts mirrored those of LaBrosse and he whispered for his travelling companion to keep going while he stopped to see what was on the sergeant's mind.

This was no time to argue. LaBrosse did as he was told and pedalled furiously away with a heavy heart, convinced that he would never see his friend and fellow agent again. But war was war and there was still much to do in Brittany. There were yet dozens of Allied aircrew waiting to be evacuated and LaBrosse would have to oversee the operations — especially now that Dumais seemed to be on the brink of being put out of commission.

LaBrosse didn't make St. Brieuc that night. Weary from his travels and disheartened by the latest turn of events, he slept in a ditch for a few hours before continuing his journey in the morning. He decided he would try to make St. Brieuc later that day and prepare to carry on the best he could without his colleague.

Miraculous Recovery

LaBrosse's dejection turned into incredulous elation as he entered St. Brieuc. There, sitting at a table at an outdoor café, two glasses of cognac in front of him, was a smiling Lucien Dumais. He nudged one of the glasses toward LaBrosse as the younger man collapsed into the chair opposite him while he fired off a staccato burst of questions.

"All he wanted was the bicycle," Dumais said with a chuckle after LaBrosse stopped for breath. The two men clinked glasses in an exuberant toast.

After several more swallows of brandy, Dumais described the scene after LaBrosse's departure. There he was standing in the roadway, wondering what to do, while the German rode off on his bicycle. Then it dawned on him. He was supposed to be a legitimate citizen of France. A German soldier had just stolen something from him. A true Frenchman would complain long and loud to the authorities about such an indignity. And that's just what he did.

LaBrosse was well aware of Dumais' temper. He was not surprised to learn the German officer his colleague complained to, at the nearest army post, believed his story, that he was an important collaborator with connections to the Gestapo. The officer quickly arranged to have Dumais driven to St. Brieuc in a German military vehicle. They must have passed LaBrosse sleeping in the ditch.

Riding the crest of this wave of good fortune, the two men returned to the task of evacuating Allied aircrew and British agents. When the last trip was made in July, their escape network had successfully repatriated close to 150 downed fliers and other Allied personnel. What's more, it happened under the very noses of the enemy. Records made public in subsequent years revealed the Germans never had an inkling that Operation Bonaparte and the Shelburn Line existed.

Chapter 8
The End of the Cross-Channel Ferry

Dumais and LaBrosse were becoming disillusioned and bitter. Their lives were constantly at risk since their return to Occupied France. They were living under assumed names. They were frequenting train stations and restaurants where German soldiers and Gestapo agents could arrest them if they made one false move. Until recently, the cause made it all worthwhile. What could be nobler than getting fugitive Allied military personnel back to England to fight another day?

With the Allied landing in Normandy, they found the need for their services diminishing. Downed fliers and escaped soldiers could simply turn themselves over to the advancing Allied troops, who would see them returned safely to their units.

Operation Bonaparte was now more of a shuttle service than an essential military exercise. It didn't help matters any when Dumais heard that his operation was referred to in London as either the Cross-Channel Ferry or the Boat Train. The final straw came when a French major, on his way to talks with Free French colleagues in London, sent word to Dumais, demanding he be picked up at his destination by car and driven to Plouha. Dumais' perverse streak got the better of him. He sent a horse and cart for the major's 80-kilometre trip. When the apoplectic officer arrived at Shelburn headquarters, he berated Dumais and the entire operation.

Did He Or Didn't He?
Dumais later told a colleague, he turned to the driver of the cart and asked him why he had brought this lunatic in instead of shooting him. "The major put his hand on my shoulder, intending to spin me round," Dumais related. "I spun around all right and, drawing the .45 Colt at my belt, I fired one shot at his head. I missed intentionally, though that was easier said than done, and he vanished into the bushes, never to be seen again."

The End of the Cross-Channel Ferry

Whether this story is real or one of the "shoulda-coulda" war stories veterans delight in telling, it serves to illustrate the point that the originators of the Shelburn Line were anxious to get on to more important things, now that their services were obviously no longer needed.

Fortunately, British Intelligence also came to the conclusion such a rescue operation was no longer a necessity with an Allied foothold established on the European continent. Dumais and LaBrosse were given orders to wrap things up.

No one could have blamed them if they had bowed to an impulse to take the last MGB out of Plouha with the rest of the evacuees. But that wasn't their style.

In fact, one of the few happy mistakes of war provided LaBrosse with the means to outfit his own *maquis* unit. He was busy at the stone farmhouse sending a wireless message while Dumais led the last group of evacuees down the hillside to Bonaparte Beach. Suddenly, he heard the heavy drone of Halifax bombers overhead and went outside to investigate.

There were, in fact, two of the Allied aircraft making a low pass over the command post. LaBrosse was savvy enough to realize immediately that the planes were searching for a pre-arranged drop zone. On instinct, he grabbed a flashlight and signalled the letters

"O.K." in Morse code at the lead aircraft as it made another pass. That was enough for the perplexed pilot, who would not have wanted to fly back to England to report he had missed the rendezvous.

Christmas In July

Both bombers made another low swoop over the area where LaBrosse was repeatedly flashing the "All Clear" signal. The night sky blossomed with white parachutes. Within minutes LaBrosse was unpacking one of 30 containers that thudded to earth. Each opened canister revealed a treasure trove of arms and ammunition. The 170-strong Plouha *maquis* was in business.

But with their mixed bag of political ideologies, there were great rivalries between neighbouring Resistance units. The supplies had been intended for another group, which now threatened dire revenge unless they got what was rightfully theirs. A quick thinking LaBrosse immediately signalled London for another drop and everyone went away happy. Everyone, that is, except the pockets of German soldiers left behind for the LaBrosse/Dumais Resistance group to mop up in several fiercely fought battles.

The two Canadian agents and their band of Underground fighters were still at it in August when an American tank squadron suddenly rolled into Plouha.

The night before, the Germans had surrounded another *maquis* cell in nearby Pielo. LaBrosse was able to talk the tank commander into diverting his squadron to the besieged village to rescue the trapped Resistance fighters. His persuasive powers were such that he and Dumais were given a ride on one of the tanks so they could take part in the counterattack.

While LaBrosse continued to fight with the local Underground until the end of the war, Dumais was tapped to work with the U.S. Army to help restore civil order, identify collaborators, and make sure the innocent were spared in the reprisals and vendettas that followed the German occupation.

One potential victim Dumais was able to assist was a local printer who had helped prepare false identification papers for Allied fugitives. Falsely accused of collaborating with the Germans, he was one step away from being executed by an angry and vengeful mob. Dumais was able to provide evidence of the man's willingness to risk his life and the lives of his family to help the Allied cause.

Well-Deserved Medals

Dumais' military career ended with the cease-fire in May 1945. By that time, he had obtained the rank of captain and proudly wore such decorations as the Military

Cross, the Military Medal, the Efficiency Medal, and the Freedom Medal.

LaBrosse rejoined the Canadian Army after the war, eventually serving with the Third Battalion of the Royal 22nd Regiment in Korea. He retired from the Canadian Armed Forces with the rank of lieutenant-colonel in 1971. Among his awards were the Military Cross, the Legion of Honour, the French Croix de Guerre (*avec palme et étoile de vermeille*), and the U.S. Medal of Liberty with silver bar.

The Shelburn Line and Operation Bonaparte were such a closely guarded secret that none of the Allied fugitives knew a network existed at the time. Most of them had figured they had merely been fortunate enough to fall into the hands of a group of French Underground fighters who knew how to get them to safety.

Only after the war was long over and secret documents were released, was it revealed that in the seven months of its existence, Shelburn rescued 307 down Allied airmen and secret agents. Bonaparte accounted for almost half this total. Of all the escape networks on the European continent, Shelburn was the most successful. Not a single "package" was lost.

The only casualty was the House of Alphonse — Operation Bonaparte's stone farmhouse command

Raymond LaBrosse and Lucien Dumais (wearing cap and
medals) salute during the playing of *O Canada* and
La marseillaise at Plouha in 1984.

post. Near the end of hostilities, a German patrol suspected the building was harbouring Resistance fighters. They burned it to the ground, bringing to an inglorious end a structure with a proud history of helping regain the freedom of close to 150 Allied service personnel stranded in Nazi-occupied France.

Epilogue
Plouha Forty Years Later

The author had the good fortune to serve as Communications Advisor to The Honourable Bennett Campbell, Canadian Minister of Veterans Affairs. His duties included accompanying the Minister on various pilgrimages to former battlefields around the world. In 1984, he was on hand in Plouha when the Minister and several of the original Operation Bonaparte participants attended a ceremony unveiling a commemorative plaque attached to one of the rocks on the rescue beach.

It was a time of great joy and great sadness. Part of the contingent included Lucien Dumais, Raymond LaBrosse, and Gaby Chartrand. Each was exuberantly embraced by former members of the French Resistance, most of whom hadn't seen their one-time comrades-in-arms in nearly 40 years.

Tears actually streamed down LaBrosse's cheeks when one of the former Resistance fighters presented

The Canadian and French flags fly over the ceremonial grounds where a plaque was unveiled to the heroes of both countries who helped Allied personnel escape from Nazi-occupied France.

him with the wireless radio he had left behind in Plouha when he returned to Canada after the war.

However, a pall of gloom hung over the huge reception room during the reunion, despite the unending flow of wine and cognac and the presentation of a large gâteau iced with cream cheese, decorated with red caviar in the shape of the Canadian maple leaf flag.

Inevitably, stories circulated of former comrades killed in the last days of the war or who had succumbed to illness since. One particularly harsh blow to those who hadn't already heard was the news about MGB 503. The Royal Navy motor gunboat that made so many successful crossings between England and Brittany, hit a mine in the English Channel in May 1945, with the loss of all 36 crew members.

But the reunion had one particularly happy story to round out the festivities. Accompanying Raymond LaBrosse on the pilgrimage, courtesy of the Ministry of Veterans Affairs, were the stationmaster's daughter LaBrosse had married in 1945 — and the LaBrosses' beautiful and grown-up daughter, Dominique.

Bibliography

Bishop, Arthur. *Unsung Courage*. Toronto: Harper-Collins Publishing Ltd., 2001.

Cosgrove, Edmund. *The Evaders*. Toronto: Clarke, Irwin & Company Limited, 1970

Dumais, Lucien. *The Man Who Went Back*. London: Leo Cooper Ltd., 1975.

Foot, M.R.D. and Langley, J.M. *MI9*. London: The Bodley Head, 1979

Lavender, Emerson and Scheffe, Norman. *The Evaders*. Toronto: McGraw Hill Ryerson, 1992

MacLaren, Roy. *Canadians Behind Enemy Lines*. Vancouver: University of British Columbia Press, 1981.

McIntosh, Dave. *High Blue Battle*. Toronto: Stoddard Publishers, 1990

Bibliography

Reader's Digest Association Ltd. *The Canadians at War: Volumes 1&2.* Montreal, 1969

Veterans Affairs Canada. *Uncommon Courage.* Minister of Supply and Services Canada, 1985

Photo Credits

Acknowledgments

The author found a wealth of information in a wide variety of books about escape and evasion during World War II. He highly recommends as interesting reading Roy MacLaren's *Canadians Behind Enemy Lines*, Arthur Bishop's *Unsung Courage*, and the Reader's Digest two-volume series *The Canadians at War*. Thanks are also due to Pat Smith of Veterans Affairs Canada, Marc Laferrière of the Department of National Defence's Directorate of History and Heritage, and friend and colleague Bob Diotte, who recently retired from DND's Communications Branch. Gratitude is also extended to The Honourable Bennett Campbell, former Veterans Affairs Minister, who made it possible for the author to attend a commemorative ceremony for the men of Operation Bonaparte in Plouha. And, finally, words cannot convey the appreciation and respect the author feels for three of the main characters in this book — Raymond LaBrosse, Lucien Dumais, and Gaby Chartrand. They graciously shared their stories with him over several days — and a glass or two of wine — during that wonderful pilgrimage to Brittany in 1984.

About the Author

Tom Douglas, an award-winning journalist and author, lives in Oakville, Ontario with his wife Gail, also an author in the Amazing Stories series. Tom's father, Sgt. H.M. (Mel) Douglas, was part of the Invasion Force that stormed the beaches of Normandy on D-Day, June 6, 1944. Tom is a member of the Royal Canadian Legion, worked as a Communications Advisor for Veterans Affairs Canada, and has written speeches for the Minister of National Defence. Recently, he self-published a book, *Some Sunny Day* about his family's experiences in Northern Ontario following his father's return from World War II.

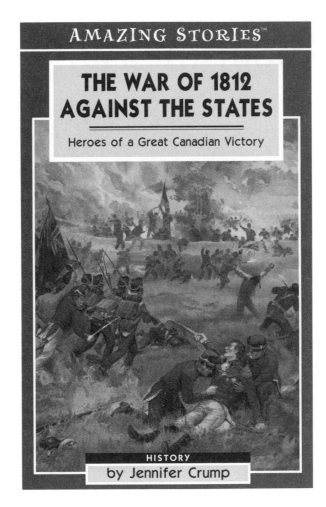

AMAZING STORIES™

THE WAR OF 1812 AGAINST THE STATES

Heroes of a Great Canadian Victory

HISTORY

by Jennifer Crump

The War of 1812
ISBN 1-55153-948-9

AMAZING STORIES™

UNSUNG HEROES OF THE ROYAL CANADIAN AIR FORCE

Incredible Tales of Courage and Daring During World War II

HISTORY

by Cynthia J. Faryon

Unsung Heroes of the RCAF
ISBN 1-55153-977-2

AMAZING STORIES™

ÉTIENNE BRÛLÉ

The Mysterious Life and Times
of an Early Canadian Legend

HISTORY/BIOGRAPHY
by Gail Douglas

Étienne Brûlé
ISBN 1-55153-961-6

AMAZING STORIES™

TOM THOMSON

The Life and Mysterious Death
of the Famous Canadian Painter

HISTORY/BIOGRAPHY

by Jim Poling Sr.

Tom Thomson
ISBN 1-55153-950-0

OTHER AMAZING STORIES

These titles are available wherever you buy books. If you have trouble finding the book you want, call the Altitude order desk at 1-800-957-6888, e-mail your request to: orderdesk@altitudepublishing.com or visit our Web site at www.amazingstories.ca

All titles retail for $9.95 Cdn or $7.95 US. (Prices subject to change.)

New AMAZING STORIES titles are published every month. If you would like more information, e-mail your name and mailing address to: amazingstories@altitudepublishing.com.